How to Protect Your Children from Child Abuse:

A Parent's Guide

Boy Scouts of America

Introduction

Our children are often faced with choices affecting their development and safety. As parents, we can do our best to provide education and guidance to prepare our children to make the best decisions. One way that we do this is to talk with our children. Some subjects are easy to discuss with our children—sports, their grades in school, their friends, and many other features of our daily lives. Other things are more difficult for us to discuss, including child abuse—especially child sexual abuse.

Although discussing child abuse with your children may be difficult for you, it is very important. Perhaps the most important step parents can take to protect their children from abuse is to have open communication in the home. Research has shown that children whose parents talk to them about preventing abuse are more effective at fending off assaults. Your role is very important.

More than three million reports of child abuse are received each year, including half a million reports of *child sexual abuse.* As a major youth-serving organization, the Boy Scouts of America has a unique opportunity to help protect the youth of our nation. This booklet is designed to give you essential information that should help you teach your children how to protect themselves.

If your son is a new Cub Scout, this might be the first time that you have seen this *Parent's Guide.* For parents who have other sons in Scouting, and for those whose sons have advanced in Cub Scouting, we hope that you are familiar with this guide and have discussed its contents with your children. In either case, we encourage you to make this information part of a continuing family effort that reinforces the concepts included in this guidebook.

We do not expect that your son will become a victim of child abuse. It is extremely important, however, that if he ever faces an abusive situation, he knows that there are adults in his life who will listen and respond in a supportive manner. The purpose of this booklet is to help you and your son establish, or reinforce, open communication on this sensitive topic.

Section I.
Information for Parents

Using This Booklet

This booklet is divided into two sections. The first section is for your information. It contains information about child abuse and provides some tips to help parents talk about child abuse with their Cub Scout–age sons. The second section is for you to share with your son. **It begins with a few simple exercises for you both to complete together as part of his requirements for the Bobcat badge**. The second section also contains some optional activities for him.

It is important that you read the entire booklet before you and your son do any of the exercises together. Once you are comfortable with the topics in this booklet, you will be able to present the information in ways he can understand. Feel free to reword an exercise in order to help your child gain a better understanding.

Child Abuse: Basic Information for Parents

An abused or neglected child is a child who is harmed, or threatened with physical or mental harm, by the acts or lack of action of a person responsible for the child's care. There are several forms of abuse: physical abuse, emotional abuse, and sexual abuse. Child neglect is a form of abuse that occurs when a person responsible for the care of a child is able, but fails, to provide necessary food, clothing, shelter, or care. Each state has its own definitions and laws concerning child abuse and child neglect.

Child abuse and neglect are serious problems for our society. The number of cases reported has increased each year since 1976, when statistics were first kept. A brief discussion of each form of abuse follows:

Neglect

A child is neglected if the persons he depends on do not provide food, clothing, shelter, medical care, education, and supervision. When these basic needs are *deliberately withheld,* not because the parents or caregivers are poor, it is considered neglect. Often parents or caregivers of neglected children are so overwhelmed by their own needs that they cannot recognize the needs of their children.

Physical Abuse

Physical abuse is the deliberate injury of a child by a person responsible for the child's care. Physical abuse often stems from unreasonable punishment, or of punishment that is too harsh for the child. Sometimes, physical abuse occurs when caregivers react to stress. Drinking and drug abuse by caretakers have become more common contributing factors in physical abuse cases.

Physical abuse injuries can include bruises, broken bones, burns, and abrasions. Children experience minor injuries as a normal part of childhood, usually in places such as the shins, knees, and elbows. When the injuries are found in soft-tissue areas on the abdomen or back, or don't seem to be typical childhood injuries, it is possible that the child has been physically abused.

Emotional Abuse

Emotional abuse is harder to recognize, but is just as harmful to the child than other forms of abuse. Emotional abuse damages the child's self-esteem and, in extreme cases, can cause developmental problems and speech disorders. A child suffers from emotional abuse when constantly ridiculed, rejected, blamed, or compared unfavorably with brothers, sisters, or other children.

Expecting too much from the child in academics, athletics, or other achievements is a common cause of emotional abuse by parents or other adults. When a child can't meet these expectations, he feels that he is never quite good enough.

Sexual Abuse

When an adult or an older child uses his or her authority over a child to involve the child in sexual activity, it is child sexual abuse, and that person is a child molester. The molester might use tricks, bribes, pressure, threats, or force to persuade the child to join in sexual activity. Sexual abuse includes any activity performed for the sexual satisfaction of the molester, including acts ranging from exposing one's sex organs (exhibitionism), observing another's sex organs or sexual activity (voyeurism), to fondling and rape.

Here are a few facts you should know about child sexual abuse:

- Child sexual abuse occurs to as many as 25 percent of girls and 14 percent of boys before they reach 18 years of age.

- Boys and girls could be sexually abused at any age; however, most sexual abuse occurs between the ages of 7 and 13.

- Eighty to 90 percent of sexually abused boys are molested by acquaintances who are nonfamily members.

- Females perform 20 percent of the sexual abuse of boys under age 14 (prepubescents).

- Children are most likely to be molested by someone they know and trust.

- Few sexually abused children tell anyone that they have been abused. Children are usually told to keep the abuse secret. This could involve threats, bribes, or physical force.

- Children might feel responsible for their abuse and fear an angry reaction from their parents.

Sexual Molestation by Peers

Approximately one-third of sexual molestation is committed by other children. If your child tells you about club initiations in which sexual activity is included, or if your child tells you about inappropriate or tricked, pressured, or forced sexual activity by other children, this is a form of sexual abuse and you need to take steps to stop the activity. This kind of sexual misconduct is serious and should not be ignored.

Children who molest other children need professional help. They are much more likely to respond to treatment when young than are adults who began in adolescence to molest children and received no treatment, and continued to do so into adulthood.

Parents and others who work with children need to distinguish between normal sexual behavior of children and abusive behavior. All children are curious about sexual behavior as a part of growing up. This behavior is not appropriate when it is forced, when the person who provokes the activity has more power, or when the sexual behavior lacks consent. When parents are concerned about their son's sexual behavior, they should try to talk with him and discuss what worries them specifically about his behavior.

Signs of Sexual Abuse

The clearest sign that a child has been sexually abused is his statement saying that he was. Children often do not tell about their abuse, however, so parents should be alert for other signs. These are some signs to watch for:

- *Hints, indirect messages*—Refusing to go to a friend's or relative's home for no apparent reason; for example, "I just don't like him anymore."

- *Seductive or provocative behavior*—Acting out adult sexual behavior or using sexual language a young child is unlikely to know.

- *Physical symptoms*—Irritation of genital or anal areas.

The following are common signs that children are upset and need parental support. They might also be signs that your child is being sexually abused:

- *Self-destructive behavior*—Using alcohol or drugs, deliberately harming himself, running away, attempting suicide, or sexual recklessness or promiscuity.

- *Unhappiness*—Undue anxiety and crying, sleep disturbances, or loss of appetite.

- *Regression*—Behaving like a younger child, thumb sucking, or bed-wetting.

- *Difficulty at school*—Sudden drop in grades, behavioral problems, or truancy.

The presence of any of these signs should not be taken as an absolute sign of sexual abuse, but, if present for longer than several days, should be a sign that your child needs your help for whatever is bothering him.

Preventing Child Abuse

Except for sexual abuse of boys, the great majority of child abuse happens within families. Preventing sexual abuse outside of the family requires a different approach than preventing abuse that involves parents. Prevention efforts for emotional and physical abuse as well as neglect generally focus on helping the abusers, often the parents, change their behavior.

Some physical and emotional abuse stems from reactions by parents to the stresses in their lives. By learning to recognize these stresses, and then taking a time-out when the pressures mount, we can avoid abusing those we love. The next page lists some alternatives to physical and emotional abuse for overstressed parents. These suggestions come from the National Committee to Prevent Child Abuse.

Alternatives to Child Abuse

The next time everyday pressures build up to the point where you feel like lashing out—**Stop!** Try any of these simple alternatives. You'll feel better . . . and so will your child:

- Take a deep breath. And another. Then remember you are the adult.

- Close your eyes and imagine you're hearing what your child is about to hear.

- Press your lips together and count to ten; or, better yet, to twenty.

- Put your child in a time-out chair. (Remember this rule: One time-out minute for each year of age.)

- Put yourself in a time-out chair. Think about why you are angry: Is it your child, or is your child simply a convenient target for your anger?

- Phone a friend.

- If someone can watch the children, go outside and take a walk.

- Splash cold water on your face.

- Hug a pillow.

- Turn on some music. Maybe even sing along.

- Pick up a pencil and write down as many *helpful* words as you can think of. Save the list.

Few parents mean to abuse their children. When parents take time out to get control of themselves before they grab hold of their children, everybody wins.

In addition to these alternatives, parents and other child caregivers may want to think about the following questions* suggested by Douglas Besharov, the first director of the U.S. National Center on Child Abuse and Neglect, regarding the ways they discipline their children.

- Is the purpose of the punishment to educate the child or to vent the parent's anger?

- Is the child capable of understanding the relationship between his behavior and the punishment?

- Is the punishment appropriate and within the bounds of acceptable discipline?

- Is a less severe, but equally effective, punishment available?

- Is the punishment degrading, brutal, or extended beyond the limits of the child's endurance?

- If physical force is used, is it done carefully to avoid injury?

These questions help to define the boundaries between acceptable discipline and child abuse. Other causes of child abuse inside the family might be much more complex and require professional help to resolve.

Preventing sexual abuse outside the family calls for a different approach. Because parents cannot guarantee a safe environment for their children outside the home, preventing sexual abuse focuses on training the youth—the potential target of the abuse—about the "three Rs" of Youth Protection: *recognizing* schemes and situations used by child molesters; *resisting* attempts of molesters; and *reporting* anyone who tries to molest.

---

*Adapted from Douglas J. Besharov. *Recognizing Child Abuse: A Guide for the Concerned.* New York: Free Press, 1990.

Talking with Your Child About Sexual Abuse

It is very difficult for many parents to talk to their children about sexual abuse. The information in this section, and the exercises in the youth section, are intended to make that task easier.

The following points should help you and your child talk about sexual abuse prevention:

• *If you feel uncomfortable discussing sexual abuse with your child, let him know.* When you feel uncomfortable discussing sexual abuse with your children and try to hide your uneasiness, your children might misinterpret the anxiety and be less likely to approach you when they need help. You can use a simple statement like, "I wish we did not have to talk about this. I am uncomfortable because I don't like to think that this could happen to you. I want you to know that it's important, and you can come to me whenever you have a question or if anybody ever tries to hurt you."

• *Select words your child understands.* One main concern of parents is finding words to explain sexual abuse. Most experts on child abuse prevention believe that children should learn the proper names for their genitalia; however, if you are uncomfortable with using the names of body parts, use whatever terms your child understands.

• *Provide the opportunity for your child to practice Youth Protection skills.* Learning is more effective when children can practice the skills they are taught. Practicing the exercise of their rights (see Section II. Information for Children) with parents gives children confidence.

Many parents feel that teaching children about sexual abuse will take away their children's innocence. Many children are at risk of sexual abuse because they do not have the maturity to understand why a child molester would want to look at, touch, or otherwise violate them. This, in part, explains why children who are sexually abused at a young age do not realize that they were abused until they are older. It also explains a child's confusion if the parents or other adults overreact when the child tells about sexual abuse.

When a Child Discloses Abuse

If your child becomes a victim of abuse, your first reaction can be very important in helping him through the ordeal. The following guidelines may help you:

- **Don't** panic or overreact to the information your child tells you.

- **Don't** criticize your child or tell your child he misunderstood what happened.

- **Do** respect your child's privacy and take your child to a place where the two of you can talk without interruptions or distractions.

- **Do** reassure your child that he is not to blame for what happened. Tell him that you appreciate being told about the incident and will help to make sure that it won't happen again.

- **Do** encourage your child to tell the proper authorities what happened, but try to avoid repeated interviews that can be stressful for the child.

- **Do** consult your health care provider or other child abuse authority about the need for medical care or counseling for your child.

> You should show real concern, but NOT alarm or anger, when questioning your child about possible child abuse.

Finally, if your child has been sexually abused, do not blame yourself or your child. People who victimize children are not easy to identify. They come from all walks of life and all socioeconomic levels. Often they have positions of status—they go to church, hold regular jobs, and are active in the community. Child molesters are sometimes very skilled at controlling and using children, often by giving them excessive attention, gifts, and money. Child molesters use their skills on parents and other adults, disguising their abusive behavior behind friendship and care for the child.

Resources

BSA Youth Protection Materials

Along with this booklet, the Boy Scouts of America has an educational video for use by Cub Scout packs or dens. This award-winning production provides age-appropriate information about sexual abuse of boys.

It Happened to Me is a video for Cub Scout–age boys that shows common situations in which sexual abuse could occur. The video discusses how child molesters often resort to tricks for gaining access to their victims. It emphasizes that if a boy has been sexually abused, he should talk to his parents or other trusted adults. The video also stresses that it is not the child's fault if he has been sexually abused. It is the child molester who is responsible.

It Happened to Me should be shown to boys 6 to 10 years of age *only* when a parent or other adult responsible for the child's care is present with the child.

This videotape is available from your BSA local council. The BSA encourages Cub Scout packs or dens to view the video annually. A meeting guide supporting the video's use can be found in the *Cub Scout Leader Book* (1994 and later editions). Copies may also be obtained from your council.

For Scouting's leaders and parents, the BSA has a video-taped training session, *Youth Protection Guidelines: Training for Volunteer Leaders and Parents,* available from your BSA local council with regular training sessions scheduled in most districts. The training addresses many questions that Scout volunteers and parents have regarding child sexual abuse.

In addition to these videotaped materials, the BSA sometimes provides Youth Protection information to its members and families through *Boys' Life* and *Scouting* magazines.

Other Sources of Child Abuse Prevention Information

National Center for Child Abuse and Neglect
U.S. Department of Health and Human Services
P.O. Box 1182
Washington, DC 20013
800-394-3366

National Committee to Prevent Child Abuse
332 South Michigan Avenue, Suite 1600
Chicago, iL 60604-4537
312-663-3520

National Center for Missing and Exploited Children
2101 Wilson Boulevard, Suite 550
Arlington, VA 22201
800-843-5678

Section II.
Information for Children

The *Child's Bill of Rights* outlines some specific ways your child can protect himself. You should discuss these and the Basic Rules of Safety for Children with your child before completing the Bobcat Youth Protection requirements. These could provide the information that your son needs to help him respond to the situations in the exercises.

Child's Bill of Rights

When feeling threatened, you have the right to

- Trust your instincts or feelings.

- Expect privacy.

- Say no to unwanted touching or affection.

- Say no to an adult's inappropriate demands and requests.

- Withhold information that could jeopardize your safety.

- Refuse gifts.

- Be rude or unhelpful if the situation warrants.

- Run, scream, and make a scene.

- Physically fight off unwanted advances.

- Ask for help.

You should remind your son that these are actions that will give him the power to protect himself, and that some of these might not be appropriate for situations where he is not threatened.

Basic Rules of Safety for Children

Cub Scout–age children benefit from having concrete safety *rules.* It is important, however, to stress that traditional cautions about "strangers" are not enough to protect our children. Children have different ideas than adults do about who a stranger might be. In addition, the person who harms a child is usually someone the child knows. It might be more helpful to teach your children to recognize possibly threatening situations or actions.

Discuss the following safety rules with your child:

• If you are in a public place and get separated from your parent (or the person in charge of you), do not wander around looking for him or her. Go to a police officer, a checkout counter, the security office, or the lost-and-found area and quickly tell someone in charge that you have been separated from your parent and need help.

• You should not get into a car or go anywhere without your parent's permission.

• Adults and older youths who are not in your family and who need help (such as finding an address or locating a lost pet) should not ask children for help; they should ask other adults.

• You should use the buddy system and try not to go anyplace alone.

• Always ask your parent's permission before going into someone else's home.

• No one should ask you to keep a special secret when someone has been scared or hurt by the secret. If this happens, tell your parent or teacher.

• If someone insists on taking your picture or videotaping you and taking your clothes off, tell your parent or teacher.

• No one should touch you in ways or places that make you feel bad. You should not touch anyone else in ways that will make them feel bad. You should ask an adult you trust questions whenever you are mixed up about someone's touch or behavior.

- You have the right to say "No!" to anyone who tries to take you somewhere, touches you, or makes you feel uncomfortable in any way.

These are some simple safety rules that can be approached in the same nonfrightening manner in which you tell your child not to play with fire. They emphasize situations common to many child molestation cases.

Personal Protection Rules for Computer On-line Services

When you're on-line, you are in a public place, among thousands of people who are on-line at the same time. Be safe by following these personal protection rules and you will have fun:

- Keep on-line chats with strangers to public places, not in e-mail.

- Do not tell anyone on-line your real last name, phone numbers at home or school, your parents' workplaces, or the name or location of your school or home address unless you have your parent's permission first. Never give your password to anyone but a parent or other adult in your family.

- If someone shows you e-mail with sayings that make you feel uncomfortable, trust your feelings. You are probably right to be watchful. Do not answer. Tell a parent what happened.

- If somebody tells you to keep what's going on between the two of you secret, tell a parent.

- Be careful whom you talk to. Anyone who starts talking about subjects that make you feel uncomfortable is probably an adult posing as a kid.

- Pay attention if someone tells you things that don't fit together. One time an on-line friend will say he or she is 12, and another time will say he or she is 14. That is a warning that this person is lying and may be an adult posing as a kid.

- Unless you talk to a parent about it first, never talk to anybody by phone if you know that person only on-line. If someone asks you to call—even if it's collect or a toll-free, 800 number—that's a warning. That person can get your phone number this way, either from a phone bill or from caller ID.

- Never agree to meet someone you have met only on-line any place off-line, in the real world.

- Watch out if someone on-line starts talking about *hacking,* or breaking onto other people's or companies' computer systems; *phreaking* (the "ph"sounds like an "f"), the illegal use of long-distance services or cellular phones; or *viruses,* on-line programs that destroy or damage data when other people download these onto their computers.

- Promise your parent or an adult family member and yourself that you will honor any rules about how much time you are allowed to spend on-line and what you do and where you go while you are on-line.

Bobcat Requirements

1. Child Abuse and Being a Good Cub Scout

When a boy joins the Cub Scouting program, he assumes a duty to be faithful to the rules of Scouting as represented in the Cub Scout Promise, Law of the Pack, and Cub Scout motto. The rules of Scouting don't require a Scout to put himself in possibly dangerous situations—quite the opposite, we want Cub Scouts to "be prepared" and to "do their best" to avoid these situations.

We hope that you will discuss these rules with your Cub Scout and be sure that he understands that he should not risk his safety to follow the rules of Cub Scouting.

Cub Scouting's Principles

The Cub Scout Promise includes the phrase, "To help other people." This means that a Cub Scout should be willing to do things for others that would please them, but only when his parent has given permission and knows where he is and who he is with.

The Law of the Pack includes the phrase, "The Cub Scout follows Akela." Akela is a good leader and should never ask you to do something that you feel bad about. If Akela, who might be a teacher, coach, or other youth leader, ever asks you to do something you think is bad, as a Cub Scout you have the right to say "No!" and tell your parents or another adult you trust.

2. What If . . .

In this activity the parent describes situations that the child should recognize as possibly dangerous. Once the parent describes a situation, the child tells or shows what he would do if ever faced with a similar situation. After each situation, some possible responses are listed.

For some of these situations you might already have set rules. You should not change your rules in response to the exercise unless there is new information that you have not previously considered. You should also feel free to reword the situation if that helps your child understand the situation better.

Situations and Suggested Actions for Each

What if you are home alone, the telephone rings, and a voice on the other end asks if your parents are home? What would you do?

• Tell the caller your parents are busy and cannot come to the phone.

• Take a message and the phone number of the caller.

• If the message needs an immediate response, call your parent.

• Do not tell the caller you are home alone.

• Let the answering machine answer and do not pick up the phone until you are sure who the caller is.

What if an adult invites you on a camping trip and suggests that you allow him to take your picture when you are not wearing clothes? What would you do?

• Tell that person you do not want to have your picture taken when you do not have your clothes on.

• When you return home, tell your parents what happened.

• Be very careful around that person in the future, and be sure to tell your parents anything that bothers you about that person.

What if a neighbor comes to you and says that your parent is sick and you must go with him or her? This neighbor is not a person you have been told it's okay to go with. What would you do?

- If you are at school, ask the principal or your teacher to help you make sure your parent really sent this person for you.

- If you are at home or somewhere else, call the emergency number your parents gave you, such as where they work, or a close relative, for help in making sure your parent sent this person.

- Do not go anywhere without checking with the person you have been told to contact in this kind of situation.

What if you are in a public rest room and someone tries to touch you in ways or places that make you feel uncomfortable? What would you do?

- Yell "STOP THAT" as loudly as you can.

- Run out of the room as quickly as possible.

- Tell your parent, a police officer, security guard, or other adult (such as your teacher) what happened.

What if you are walking to school in the rain and a car stops and the driver asks if you want a ride? What would you do?

- Stay away from the car. You do not need to get close to the car to answer.

- Unless you have your parent's permission to ride with the person, say "No, thank you." If the driver keeps asking, say "No!," then get away.

- Tell your teacher when you get to school and tell your parent when you get home.

What if you are playing on the playground and an adult comes up to you and asks you to help find his or her lost puppy? What would you do?

- If you do not know the person, stay away and tell a teacher or other adult you trust.

- Adults should ask other adults for help. Before you help that person, you must get your parent's permission.

- Tell your parent what happened.

What if you are walking down the street and an elderly neighbor tells you that you'll get a quarter to help carry groceries? The person asks you to come into his or her house. What would you do?

- Get permission first.

- Do not ever go into anyone else's house without your parent's permission.

- Tell your parent about the person.

What if an older child you know invites you to play a game, and to pretend that he or she is the doctor and you are the patient? This child tells you to take off all of your clothes so that the "doctor" can examine the "patient." What would you do?

- Keep your clothes on.

- If he or she persists, say "No!," then yell and get away.

- Tell your parent.

Other Youth Protection Activities (Not Part of the Bobcat Requirements)

My Safety Notebook

This exercise will help your child avoid situations that could lead to abuse or molestation. The safety notebook can be a loose-leaf notebook or pages stapled together for which your child has made an original cover. (Elective 9: Art, Bear Cub Scout requirements; Artist activity badge, Webelos Scout requirements.)

This safety notebook gives your child a place to list emergency telephone numbers, including parents' work numbers and a neighbor or friend's number to call when parents are unavailable. (Achievement 4: Know Your Home and Community, Wolf Cub Scout requirements.) In addition, your child can list the safety rules that you and he have discussed together. Encourage your child to decorate each page with pictures and drawings that illustrate some of the rules.

He may also want to list other kinds of safety guidelines, such as rules for bicycle safety. (Achievement 9: Be Safe at Home and on the Street, Wolf Cub Scout requirements. Achievement 14: Ride Right, Bear Cub Scout requirements; Readyman activity badge, Webelos Scout requirements.)

"My Safety Notebook" is intended to be a fun activity for getting across some serious concerns. It is a personalized reference that can reassure your child that he knows how to respond when confronted by a potentially dangerous situation.

Plays and Skits

Sometimes children enjoy creating a script for a play or skit that will dramatize their understanding of the safety rules. The skit could then be presented to other children as a service project. (Showman activity badge, Webelos Scout requirements; Elective 2: Be an Actor, Wolf Cub Scout requirements.) As a parent, you can guide the creation of the script so that the situations reflect an understanding of the rules and give an opportunity for practicing the skills. Children need to feel that they can protect themselves.

As pointed out earlier, children learn Youth Protection strategies better and are able to apply them when necessary if they practice these skills.

Family Meeting

A child must feel comfortable telling his parent about any sensitive problems or experiences in which someone approached him in an improper manner, or in a way that made him feel uncomfortable. Studies have shown that more than half of all child abuse incidents are never reported because the victims are too afraid or too confused to report their experiences.

Your children need to be allowed to talk freely about their likes and dislikes, their friends, and their true feelings. You can create open communication through family meetings where safety issues can be talked about by the entire family. (Family Member activity badge, Webelos Scout requirements.) Some of the activities suggested here could be done in the setting of a family meeting.

No. 46-014

Boy Scouts of America

1999 Printing

Welcome to the
BEAR
Cub Scout Book!

Contents

Illustrations of Baloo by Robert Depew

33107
ISBN 0-8395-3107-9
© 1998 Boy Scouts of America
Revised 1999

10 9 8 7 6 5 4 3 2 1

Parent Guide _____

If you could give your boy the greatest gift of all, what would it be? It wouldn't be money or anything money can buy. Whether you are rich or poor, the greatest gift is within your power because that gift is helping a boy become a person with a good feeling about himself and a genuine concern for others. Cub Scouting can help you provide this gift.

Your Son, Scouting, and You

As a parent, you want your son to grow up to be self-reliant and dependable—a person of worth, a caring individual. Scouting has these same goals in mind for him.

Since 1910 we've been weaving lifetime values into fun and educational activities designed to help parents teach their sons how to make good decisions throughout their lives and give them confidence as they become the adult leaders of tomorrow.

In a society where your son is often taught that winning is everything, Cub Scouting teaches him to *do his best* and *be helpful to others* as expressed in the Cub Scout Promise, motto, and Law of the Pack.

A Cub Scout den will involve your boy in a group of boys his own age where he can earn status and recognition. There he will also gain a sense of personal achievement from the new skills he learns.

The Purposes of Cub Scouting

Cub Scouting is the phase of the program offered by the Boy Scouts of America for first- through fifth-grade (or 7-, 8-, 9-, and 10-year-old) boys. The purposes of Cub Scouting are to help parents and community organizations help boys by

- Positively influencing character development and encouraging spiritual growth

- Helping boys develop habits and attitudes of good citizenship

- Encouraging good sportsmanship and pride in growing strong in mind and body

- Improving understanding within the family

- Strengthening the ability to get along with other boys and to respect other people

- Fostering a sense of personal achievement by helping boys develop new interests and skills

- Showing how to be helpful and do one's best

- Providing fun and exciting new things to do

- Preparing boys to become Boy Scouts

Cub Scouting

Your Cub Scout is a member of a den. Most dens have six to eight boys in them and meet once a week. Den meetings are a time for learning new things and having fun. Dens are led by a team of adult volunteers—the den leader and assistant den leader(s). Den leaders are usually parents of boys in the den.

Your Cub Scout is also a member of a pack. Packs consist of several dens. Most packs meet once a month. Pack meetings usually follow a suggested theme and are a time for boys to be recognized for their accomplishments during the month, to perform skits and songs they've learned in den meetings, and to have fun with the entire family.

Packs are led by a Cubmaster and pack committee. Like the den leaders, the Cubmaster and assistants are volunteers and are usually parents of boys in the pack. Most pack committees consist of parents and members of the pack's chartered organization. The pack committee makes plans for pack meetings and activities and takes care of the "business" items necessary for a quality pack program.

The pack is owned by a community organization that is granted a charter by the Boy Scouts of America to use the Scouting program. This chartered organization might be a school, service club, religious group, or other group interested in youth. The chartered organization approves the leadership of the pack, provides a meeting place, and operates the pack within the guidelines and policies of the organization and the Boy Scouts of America.

Akela's OK

As you look through this book, you'll see places for "Akela's OK." That usually means your okay. Akela (ah-KAY-la) is the boy's leader. At home, that is you; at den meetings, it is the den leader; at school, it is the teacher. Almost all electives and achievements are done by you and your Cub Scout at home, not in the den meeting. This book is filled with more than two hundred pages of activities for you and your son to enjoy together. Once your Cub Scout has done his best, you can approve the completion of the requirement and the den leader will record his progress in the den records.

[date here] / *David Gilbreath*

_____ Bear credit
_____ Date and signature for
_____ Arrow point credit

The Bobcat Trail

In Rudyard Kipling's story in *The Jungle Book,* the black panther Bagheera is the mighty hunter who teaches the cubs the skills of the jungle. In Cub Scouting we use the symbol of the Bobcat. You'll find his trail on pages 15 through 21. Along this trail are the Cub Scout Promise, the Law of the Pack, and the Cub Scout motto. These are the three most important things a boy must learn because they will help him through all of the trails of Scouting.

One part of the Bobcat trail is to read and complete the exercises in the booklet *How to Protect Your Children from Child Abuse.* Child abuse is a problem in our society, and this booklet will help you help your child to avoid potentially abusive situations.

When you and your boy have followed the eight tracks of the Bobcat, your boy may wear his Bobcat badge. It will be presented at the pack meeting.

The Bear Trail

After your Cub Scout has earned his Bobcat badge, he can start along the Bear trail. This is a big adventure for a boy, one the Boy Scouts of America hopes all boys will complete. The Bobcat trail has only eight tracks; the Bear trail is much longer. The Bear trail has twenty-four achievements, twelve of which a boy must complete to earn the Bear badge.

When you have okayed the proper achievements, he may become a Bear Cub Scout. How quickly your boy progresses is up to him—and you. He should do his best to complete each achievement. That's part of the promise he made to become a Bobcat, and it is the Cub Scout motto—Do Your Best. Don't okay an achievement if you both know that he can do a better job. Go on to something else, and then go back and try again.

The important thing is to keep him interested by working on the trail with him as often as possible.

Progress Toward Ranks

Your boy doesn't have to wait until he completes his entire Bear trail before being recognized for his work. When he completes any three achievements, his den leader can present the Progress Toward Ranks emblem to him (or if he was a Wolf, he can add to his current emblem). It's a diamond-shaped emblem with a plastic thong attached, and it's worn on the right pocket button of his uniform shirt. Each time he completes three achievements, he will receive a red bead. After he gets his fourth red bead, he will be ready to receive his Bear badge at a pack meeting.

The Arrow Point Trail

Your Cub Scout can also search the Arrow Point trail. On the Bear trail, the main sections were called *achievements*, things that we would like all boys to do. On the Arrow Point trail, the main sections are called *electives*, choices that a boy can make on his own and with your guidance. Also, any achievement requirements that a boy did not use to earn the Bear badge can be used as electives toward Arrow Points.

When your Bear Cub Scout has completed his first ten electives, he will be eligible for a Gold Arrow Point. For every ten additional electives he completes, the Bear Cub Scout qualifies for a Silver Arrow Point to wear beneath the Gold. He can earn as many Silver Arrow Points as he wants until he completes the third grade (or turns 10). Arrow Points are presented at a pack meeting after he receives his Bear badge.

Do Your Best

When has a boy completed an elective or achievement? When he, in your opinion as Akela, has completed the skill to the best of his ability. In Cub Scouting, boys are judged against their own standard, not against other boys.

If your Cub Scout has a mental or physical disability that prevents him from attempting an achievement, talk to your Cubmaster about using an elective as an alternative.

The Boy Scouts of America hereby authorizes you who have read this Parent Guide to act as Akela and to indicate your willingness to serve by signing below.

I/We will be Akela in this
Bear Cub Scout Book:

Signature _____ Date _____

Signature _____ Date _____

Signature _____ Date _____

Welcome to the Bear Trail

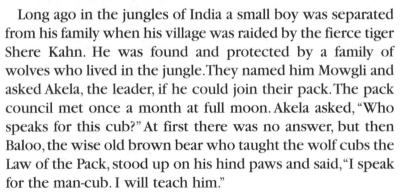

Read the next few pages in your new Cub Scout book. Find out how Baloo helped Mowgli learn the Law of the Pack.

How Baloo Taught Mowgli the Law of the Pack

Long ago in the jungles of India a small boy was separated from his family when his village was raided by the fierce tiger Shere Kahn. He was found and protected by a family of wolves who lived in the jungle. They named him Mowgli and asked Akela, the leader, if he could join their pack. The pack council met once a month at full moon. Akela asked, "Who speaks for this cub?" At first there was no answer, but then Baloo, the wise old brown bear who taught the wolf cubs the Law of the Pack, stood up on his hind paws and said, "I speak for the man-cub. I will teach him."

Bagheera, the black panther, slipped into the council ring and said, "I, too, speak for the man-cub." Shere Kahn snarled in rage. This is how Mowgli came to live with the wolf family in the jungle and learned the ways of a wolf cub.

As Mowgli grew older, Baloo taught him the Law of the Pack and the secret master words that let him talk to the other jungle creatures—all except the Bandar-log, the monkey people who did not obey the Law of the Pack. They had decided to make their own law and thought it would be a fine idea to capture Mowgli and make him their leader. They were so thoughtless and silly the other animals paid no attention to them.

The Bandar-log grabbed Mowgli one day while he was taking a nap. They carried him high above the trees to a deserted village where none of the other jungle creatures lived. While he was being carried through the branches, Mowgli called for help. Chil, the kite (hawk), heard him call and flew swiftly to tell Baloo and Bagheera.

Baloo and Bagheera were furious. They could not follow through the treetops, but they set out on foot through the jungle to rescue Mowgli. Baloo knew that the Bandar-log's greatest fear was of Kaa, the 30-foot-long python. "He can climb as well as they can. Let us go to Kaa," Baloo said.

"What can he do?" asked Bagheera. "He is not of our tribe, and he has the most evil eyes."

"He is old and cunning. Above all, he is always hungry," said Baloo hopefully.

Kaa agreed to help, and the three set off to find Mowgli. They reached the village at nightfall. Bagheera and Baloo moved in first. The Bandar-log swarmed over them, biting and scratching, for the monkey people are brave only when the odds are in their favor. Things were going badly for Baloo and Bagheera when Kaa appeared. Baloo was right; the Bandar-log were terribly frightened of Kaa. Some of them climbed the walls and towers of the city, trying to get as far away as possible; some froze in terror. Kaa battered through the wall of the ancient building where Mowgli was being held captive and set him free.

Kaa began weaving in his hunger dance, making all who watched—the Bandar-log, Baloo, and Bagheera—helpless to move. Mowgli shook his friends who were falling under Kaa's spell and woke them just in time. The three made their escape back to their own part of the jungle.

Mowgli had learned to live as a wolf cub and had begun to learn the wisdom of the bear, but he needed older friends to teach him things that would protect him. Like Mowgli, you can call on parents and leaders to help you.

The Bobcat Trail

WOLF

BOBCAT

If you were a Wolf last year, you will remember "The Story of Akela and Mowgli." If this is your first year as a Cub Scout, Baloo hopes you liked his story.

When you join the Cub Scouts, no matter how old you are you become a Bobcat first.

---

1   **Learn the CUB SCOUT PROMISE and tell what it means.**

"I, <u>Thomas</u>, promise to do my best to do my duty to God and my country, to help other people, and to obey the Law of the Pack."

EXPLAINING THE PROMISE

Promise . . . To promise means you will keep your word when you tell someone you will do something. People will trust you when you keep your promises.

Do my best . . . We are not all alike, so when we do our best it means that we have tried as hard as we can.

Do my duty …We know what is right and what is wrong, so we know what we should do at all times. When we do our duty to God, this means we practice our religion at home and at our place of worship. When we do our duty to our country, we stand up for our country. Be proud that you are an American. Stand up for your rights and the rights of all Americans.

Help other people … Do things for people even when you are not asked. Be good to people; help them and don't expect to be rewarded.

Obey the Law of the Pack … Be a good Cub Scout and be proud that you are one.

| **2** | **Learn the LAW OF THE PACK and tell what it means.** |

"The Cub Scout follows Akela. The Cub Scout helps the pack go. The pack helps the Cub Scout grow. The Cub Scout gives goodwill."

Remember Akela (ah-KAY-la) in the story? Akela is a Cub Scout name for a good leader. This can be your father, mother, guardian, aunt, uncle, grandparent, teacher, den leader, Cubmaster, or den chief. Cub Scouts learn to be good leaders. To be a good leader you must also learn to follow good leaders and learn from them.

EXPLAINING THE LAW OF THE PACK

Helps the pack go … You should go to den meetings and pack meetings and help your den in work and play. Help your pack in goodwill efforts and money-earning projects.

Helps the Cub Scout grow . . . The pack gives you a chance to learn new skills and to meet new friends. The pack also gives you a chance to be proud of yourself when you earn each new rank.

Gives goodwill . . . A Cub Scout is kind and thinks about making other people happy.

3 | **Tell what WEBELOS means.**

Webelos (WEE-buh-lows) has a secret meaning for Cub Scouts— **We**'ll **Be** **Lo**yal **S**couts. *Loyal* means that you will keep your Cub Scout Promise.

4 | **Make the CUB SCOUT SIGN and tell what it means.**

Make this sign with your right hand. Hold your arm up straight. Do not bend your elbow.

The two fingers stand for the two points of the Promise—to help other people and to obey. They look like a wolf's ears ready to listen to Akela.

When you say the Cub Scout Promise or the Law of the Pack, give the Cub Scout sign. This is the sign of Cub Scouts all over the world.

5 Make the CUB SCOUT HANDSHAKE and tell what it means.

When you shake hands, use your right hand. Put the first two fingers along the inside of your friend's wrist. This means that you are brothers in Cub Scouting and that both of you help other people and obey the Law of the Pack.

6 Say the CUB SCOUT MOTTO.

DO YOUR BEST

Do Your Best. This means to try as hard as you can in everything you do.

7 Give the CUB SCOUT SALUTE and tell what it means.

The Cub Scout salute means you respect our country's flag. Salute with your right hand. If you are wearing your Cub Scout cap, place your two fingers on the brim. If you do not have a cap, place your two fingers over your eyebrow.

8 With your parent or guardian, complete the exercises in the booklet *How to Protect Your Children from Child Abuse.*

BOBCAT

NOW YOU CAN
BECOME A BOBCAT CUB SCOUT.

_____ / _____ Date and signature for
completion of Bobcat requirements

Your Den, Pack, and Uniform

A group of Cub Scouts, called a **den**, usually meets once a week in the same place. The dens all get together once a month for a pack meeting. Remember, as a Bear Cub Scout, you are a member of a pack. Remember, too, the Law of the Pack: "The Cub Scout helps the pack go." You should bring your whole family with you to each pack meeting. You will be proud not only to have them there to see you and your friends having fun but also to have them take part in the ceremony when you have earned a badge. The badge is given to an adult member of your family, and he or she will in turn give it to you in front of the whole pack. This is a way of saying "thank you" to your family for their help in earning your award.

Now that you are a Cub Scout in the Bear program, you have a blue neckerchief to wear with your Cub Scout uniform. Don't forget your cap; it's fun to wear! If you don't wear your uniform to den and pack meetings, and on outings and special events, no one will be able to tell that you are a Cub Scout and that you have earned all the badges on your

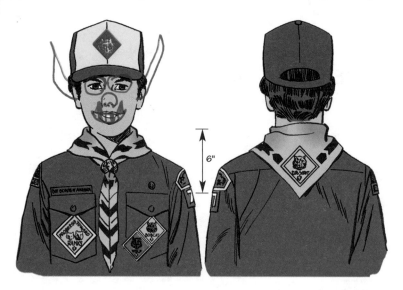

6"

uniform shirt. Be proud to wear the Cub Scout uniform. Did you know there are Cub Scouts all around the world? You are a member of a large group of boys your age.

There are year pins, temporary patches (such as the World Conservation Award), Summertime Pack Award pins, Quality Unit emblems, and lots of other awards you can earn and wear on your uniform. (Ask your den leader to help you earn them and show you where each is worn.)

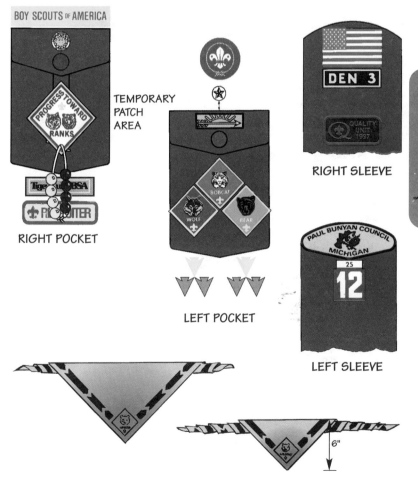

BOY SCOUTS OF AMERICA

TEMPORARY PATCH AREA

RIGHT POCKET

LEFT POCKET

RIGHT SLEEVE

LEFT SLEEVE

6"

The Bobcat Trail

The Bear Trail

You must complete twelve achievements to be a Bear Cub Scout. You can pick the ones you want to do from four different groups. You have a wide choice because there are twenty-four to pick from.

GOD (Do one.)

✓ 1. Ways We Worship

2. Emblems of Faith

COUNTRY (Do three.)

3. What Makes America Special?

4. Tall Tales

5. Sharing Your World with Wildlife

6. Take Care of Your Planet

7. Law Enforcement Is a Big Job

FAMILY (Do four.)

8. The Past Is Exciting and Important

9. What's Cooking?

10. Family Fun

11. Be Ready

12. Family Outdoor Adventures

13. Saving Well, Spending Well

SELF (Do four.)

14. Ride Right
15. Games, Games, Games!
16. Building Muscles
17. Information, Please
18. Jot It Down
19. Shavings and Chips
20. Sawdust and Nails
21. Build a Model
22. Tying It All Up
23. Sports, Sports, Sports!
24. Be a Leader

When you finish an achievement, you will need to have an adult member of your family sign and date your book. You will then take your book to the next den meeting, and your den leader will record it on the Cub Scout Den Advancement Chart and initial your book.

When you have done twelve Bear achievements, you become a Bear Cub Scout. You will get your Bear badge from an adult member of your family at the pack meeting. You may count any extra achievement requirements you earn as Arrow Point credits. Have them signed and dated.

Ways We Worship

We are lucky. The people who wrote and signed our Constitution were very wise. They understood the need of Americans to worship God as they choose. A member of your family will be able to talk with you about your duty to God. Remember, this achievement is part of your Cub Scout Promise:

I,_____, promise to do my best to do my duty to God and my country..."

Achievement 1

REQUIREMENT

> Practice your religion as you are taught in your home, church, synagogue, mosque, or other religious community.

I worship God

in song

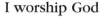

in prayer

in study

and by kind and thoughtful acts toward others.

CUB SCOUT LEADER BALOO SAYS: When you have done this requirement, have a parent or an adult sign here.

10/11/01 / _____ Date and signature for achievement 1
—OR—

_____/_____ Date and signature for Arrow Point credit

Achievements

Emblems of Faith

Many signs remind us of God. Among them are a six-pointed star, a cross, and a crescent. There are many other religious symbols. One of them might appear on a special emblem you may earn to wear on your uniform.

Learn more about your faith from your rabbi, minister, priest, imam, elder, or other religious leader.

REQUIREMENT

> ## Earn the religious emblem of your faith.

ALEPH
for Cub Scouts who
are Jewish

BISMILLAH
for Islamic Cub
Scouts

DHARMA
for Cub Scouts
who are Hindu

FAITH IN GOD
for Cub Scouts who are
members of the Church of
Jesus Christ of Latter-day
Saints (must be 9 years of
age to receive)

GOD AND COUNTRY
for Cub Scouts who are
members of the First
Church of Christ,
Scientist

GOD AND ME
for Cub Scouts who
are Protestant

JOYFUL SERVANT
for Cub Scouts
of the
Churches of Christ

LOVE FOR GOD
for Cub Scouts
of the Meher
Baba faith

LOVE OF GOD
for Polish National
Catholic Cub Scouts

Achievements

METTA
for Cub Scouts who are
Buddhist

UNITY OF MANKIND
for Cub Scouts of the
Baha'i faith

SAINT GEORGE
for Eastern Orthodox
Cub Scouts

SAINT GREGORY
for Cub Scouts who are
members of the Diocese
of the Armenian Church
of America

THAT OF GOD
for Cub Scouts of the
Religious Society of
Friends (Quakers)

PARVULI DEI
for Cub Scouts who
are Roman Catholic or
Eastern-Rite Catholic
(grades 3–5)

The Cub Scout who has earned
the religious emblem of his faith
may wear the religious emblems
square knot on his uniform, above
the left pocket.

Achievements

Ask your religious leader or local council service center for more information on religious emblems available to Cub Scouts.

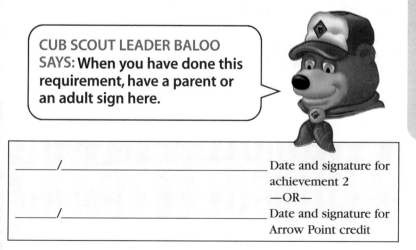

CUB SCOUT LEADER BALOO SAYS: When you have done this requirement, have a parent or an adult sign here.

_____/_____ Date and signature for
achievement 2
—OR—
_____/_____ Date and signature for
Arrow Point credit

What Makes America Special?

Americans believe everyone should be free and should control his or her own life. We have the right to own property and to worship any way we want. Our laws protect each of us equally.

People did not always live this way. How men and women got together and started our free way of life makes an interesting story.

The story is still being written. Probably your parents and grandparents and even your great-grandparents are a part of it. You can be part of it, too.

As a Cub Scout, you can be one of the reasons that America is special. Help others. Be a good citizen. Take part in the life of your country.

REQUIREMENTS

Do requirement *a* and any three of the other six requirements.

> **a. Write or tell what makes America special to you.**

America, the beautiful, is special because of its

Opportunities

People

Achievements

Freedom

_____ Bear credit
_____ / _____ Date and signature for
_____ Arrow point credit

b. With the help of your family or den leader, find out about two famous Americans. Tell the things they did or are doing to improve our way of life.

Look for great Americans in

Books

Newspapers and magazines

TV programs about
real people

There might be a great American living
in your neighborhood or community.

_____ Bear credit
_____ / _____ Date and signature for
_____ Arrow point credit

Achievements

> **c. Find out something about the old homes near where you live. Go and see two of them.**

_____ Bear credit
_____ / _____ Date and signature for
_____ Arrow point credit

> **d. Find out where places of historical interest are located in or near your town or city. Go and visit one of them with your family or den.**

These might be battlefields, monuments, or buildings or a place where a famous story or poem was written.

_____ Bear credit
_____ / _____ Date and signature for
_____ Arrow point credit

Achievements

> **e. Choose a state; it can be your favorite one or your home state. Name its state bird, tree, and flower. Describe its flag. Give the date it was admitted to the Union.**

Use a reference book to find this information:

State bird _____

State tree _____

State flower _____

Date admitted to the union _____

Sketch your
state flag.

_____ Bear credit

_____ /_____ Date and signature for

_____ Arrow point credit

> **f. Be a member of the color guard in a flag ceremony for your den or pack.**

A color guard usually has four Cub Scouts. Numbers 1 and 4 are the guards. Number 2 carries the U.S. flag. Number 3 carries the den or pack flag.

_____ Bear credit

_____ /_____ Date and signature for

_____ Arrow point credit

> **g. Display the U.S. flag in your home or fly it on three national holidays.**

Memorial Day, the last Monday in May, honors those who died in defense of our country.

Flag Day, June 14, marks the day in 1777 when Congress adopted the Stars and Stripes as our flag.

Independence Day, July 4, celebrates the adoption of the Declaration of Independence, which marked the beginning of our nation's independence from Great Britain.

Veterans Day, November 11, honors the living veterans of all our wars. It is the anniversary of the end of World War I in 1918.

Labor Day, the first Monday in September, honors all working men and women.

_____ Bear credit

_____ / _____ Date and signature for

_____ Arrow point credit

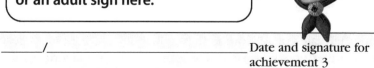

CUB SCOUT LEADER BALOO SAYS:
When you have done requirement *a* and three others, have a parent or an adult sign here.

_____ / _____ Date and signature for achievement 3

Tall Tales

A modern-day tall tale might be a fisherman's story about "the big one that got away." What we mean by "tall tales" in the *Bear Book* are stories, customs, songs, and sayings from our American past. These are handed down by families or groups of people. They tell us about the life and spirit of our ancestors. American folklore is told in stories and songs, some true and some told in a way to make the story better. One thing you can count on about tall tales or folklore is they tell about the happiness, fears, dreams, and hopes of early Americans. American folklore is full of wonderful people and adventures.

The Bear Trail • Country

REQUIREMENTS

Do all three requirements.

> **a. Tell in your own words what folklore is. List some folk-lore stories, folk songs, or historical legends from your own state or part of the country.**

SASQUATCH or BIGFOOT
A giant humanlike creature of the Pacific Northwest. Huge footprints and fleeting glimpses are all that anyone has seen of it.

PONY EXPRESS RIDERS
Between 1860 and 1861, riders carried the mail from Missouri to California. They rode at a gallop for 2,000 miles, changing horses every 10 miles.

PAUL BUNYAN
A tall-tales lumberman who leveled a forest with one swing of his ax. Then he trimmed the trees and stacked the logs for Babe, the blue ox, who swooshed them out of the woods in one haul.

PECOS BILL
A tall-tales cowboy who was raised by coyotes. He fought a 10-foot rattlesnake, tamed it, and used it as a whip. He caught and rode a mountain lion like a horse and he staked out New Mexico and dug the Grand Canyon.

Achievements

RIP VAN WINKLE

The hero of Washington Irving's story about a man who went into the mountains to hunt. There he found a group of little men playing ninepins. He joined them and after the game laid down to take a nap, which lasted 20 years.

HIAWATHA

The main character of Longfellow's poem about an American Indian chief:

You shall hear how Hiawatha
Prayed and fasted in the forest,
Not for triumphs in the battle,
And renown among the warriors,
But for profit of the people
For advantage of the nations.

CHARLIE PARKHURST

A stagecoach driver before there were railroads. Charlie was unusual, because Charlie was a lady.

THE LOST DUTCHMAN

A mine, not a man, that is still lost. Somewhere in the Superstition Mountains of Arizona there is a hole in the ground loaded with gold.

Achievements

JOHNNY APPLESEED

Jonathan Chapman was his real name. A Christian missionary who planted orchards in the wilderness, he was a friend of the American Indians and settlers. During the War of 1812 he saved the settlers from a surprise attack.

DANIEL BOONE

Hunter, pioneer, and trailblazer who led settlers over the Allegheny Mountains into Kentucky. Some say he was part man, part horse, and part alligator.

DAVY CROCKETT

Backwoods hero, member of Congress, and one of the defenders of the Alamo who died in its defense.

Achievements

JOHN HENRY

A steel-driving champion whose record has never been equaled. In 35 minutes John Henry drove two 7-foot shafts into solid rock while a steam drill made only one 9-foot shaft.

ZORRO

A hero who lived on his father's hacienda (large ranch) in southern California when it was a colony of Mexico ruled by a governor who taxed and oppressed the people. Hiding his identity behind the mask of Zorro, Don Diego would ride to protect the cruel governor's victims.

EL DORADO

The American Indians told the Spaniards that somewhere in the West was a fabulous city of gold.

BARBARA FRIETCHIE

Took up the flag hauled down by Confederate soldiers and defied Stonewall Jackson. "Shoot, if you must, this old gray head, but spare your country's flag," she said. A poem by John Greenleaf Whittier.

OLD STORMALONG

A tall-tales sailor who grew tired of the sea and said he was going to put his oar on his shoulder and walk west until someone asked: "What's that funny-looking stick on your shoulder?" There he vowed to settle down.

Achievements

ICHABOD CRANE

An awkward schoolmaster in Washington Irving's "The Legend of Sleepy Hollow" who was scared out of town on Halloween night by the ghostly headless horseman (who was not really a ghost, but a jealous rival dressed as the horseman).

MOLLY BROWN

A tough frontier lady from the Colorado silver-mining town of Leadville who helped save some of the survivors of the *Titanic*.

KING KAMEHAMEHA

For 37 years, the ruler of Hawaii long before Hawaii was a part of the United States. He began his rule in 1782 and died in 1819.

Achievements

CASEY JONES

A famous engineer who stayed with his train to warn others that it was going to crash. He died with one hand on the whistle and one hand on the brake. Old 638 crashed into a freight train that had not cleared the siding.

Folklore Match Game

1. Sasquatch or Bigfoot   ____ Was of royal blood.
2. Pony Express Riders   ____ Slept a long time.
3. Paul Bunyan   ____ She drove a stagecoach.
4. Pecos Bill   ____ Stood up to Stonewall.
5. Johnny Appleseed   ____ Was frightened by some body.
6. Daniel Boone   ____ Built of a precious metal.
7. Davy Crockett   ____ Died in the Alamo.
8. John Henry   ____ From Leadville to the *Titanic*.
9. Zorro   ____ Got tired of the sea.
10. El Dorado   ____ Beat a machine.
11. Barbara Frietchie   ____ Protected victims of a cruel governor.
12. Old Stormalong   ____ Warned the settlers of an attack.
13. Molly Brown   ____ Is famous in Kentucky.
14. Ichabod Crane   ____ A missing mine.
15. Rip Van Winkle   ____ Leveled a forest with one swing of his ax.
16. Hiawatha   ____ Rode a strange "horse."
17. Charlie Parkhurst   ____ Longfellow's chief.
18. Lost Dutchman   ____ Stayed with his train.
19. King Kamehameha   ____ Isn't a man, but a something.
20. Casey Jones   ____ Carried the mail.

b. Name at least five stories about American folklore. Point out on a United States map where they happened.

_____ Bear credit
_____ /_____ Date and signature for
_____ Arrow point credit

c. Read two folklore stories and tell your favorite one to your den.

Den leader's initials _____

_____ Bear credit
_____ /_____ Date and signature for
_____ Arrow point credit

CUB SCOUT LEADER BALOO SAYS:
When you have done all three requirements, have a parent or an adult sign here.

_____ /_____ Date and signature for achievement 4

Sharing Your World with Wildlife

Achievement 5

Every living creature has a place in this world, and there is room for all of us. Birds, fish, and animals need clean water, food, and air, just as Cub Scouts do.

You can help protect wildlife by following the fishing and hunting laws. Keep wildlife areas beautiful. Pick up trash along trails, streams, and lakeshores. Put it in trash barrels where it belongs.

This achievement is also part of the World Conservation Award (see page 259). NOTE for Akela: Also see the pages on wildlife conservation in the *Cub Scout Academics and Sports Program Guide*.

REQUIREMENTS

Do four of the following requirements:

> **a. Choose a bird or animal that you like and find out how it lives. Make a poster showing what you have learned.**

Get to know birds or animals by

Reading about them

Watching them

b. Build or make a bird feeder or birdhouse.

Use white pine or cedar lumber. Do not use pressure-treated wood.

BIRDHOUSES

Birds that nest in the hollows of trees will nest in birdhouses. Six of the more common ones are bluebirds, chickadees, titmice, nuthatches, wrens, and house finches.

Birdhouse Sizes

BIRD	FLOOR	DEPTH	HOLE ABOVE FLOOR	HOLE SIZE	PLACE ABOVE GROUND
Bluebird	5x5 in.	8 in.	6 in.	1½ in.	5-10 ft.
Chickadee	4x4 in.	8-10 in.	6-8 in.	1½ in.	6-15 ft.
Titmouse	4x4 in.	8-10 in.	6-8 in.	1¼ in.	6-15 ft.
Nuthatch	4x4 in.	8-0 in	6-8 in.	1¼ in.	12-20 ft.
Wren	4x4 in.	6-8 in.	4-6 in.	1-1¼ in.	6-10 ft.
House finch	6x6 in.	6 in.	4 in.	2 in.	8-12 ft.

_____ Bear credit

_____ /_____ Date and signature for

_____ Arrow point credit

c. Explain what a wildlife conservation officer does.

Contact a conservation officer from your state or federal fish and wildlife service. Look in your phone book. Tell the officer that you are a Cub Scout and are working on this achievement. The person you talk with might be one or more of these three things:

RESEARCHER
Studies the lives and habits of wild animals and birds. Finds out how wild things live, where they live, what they eat, what eats them, how they raise babies, and how they survive during the winter.

MANAGER
Helps provide wild animals with things they need—food, water, shelter, and living space.

EDUCATOR
Writes articles for newspapers about wildlife. He or she might be on radio or TV shows, make movies, or give talks to Cub Scout packs or school classes on wildlife.

_____ Bear credit
_____ /_____ Date and signature for
_____ Arrow point credit

Achievements

_____ Zoo   _____ Wildlife refuge
_____ Nature center   _____ Game preserve

Find out if any of these places are near your home. Take a trip to one of them with your family or den.

_____ Bear credit

_____ / _____ Date and signature for

_____ Arrow point credit

Achievements

e. Name one animal that has become extinct in the last 100 years. Tell why animals become extinct. Name one animal that is on the endangered species list.

Talk with a conservation officer or librarian.

_____ Bear credit
_____ /_____ Date and signature for
_____ Arrow point credit

CUB SCOUT LEADER BALOO SAYS:
When you have done four
requirements, have a parent or
an adult sign here.

_____ /_____ Date and signature for
achievement 5

Take Care of Your Planet

The Earth is your planet. This means that you have to help take care of it. It's the only planet we have. Conserve energy. Save our natural resources. Plant trees and flowers.

REQUIREMENTS

Do three of the following requirements:

> **a. Save 5 pounds of glass or aluminum or 1 month of daily newspapers. Turn them in at a recycling center or use your community's recycling service.**

Separate your trash at home.

Stack and tie newspapers.

Rinse bottles and aluminum cans. To save space, crush aluminum cans.

_____ Bear credit

_____ /_____ Date and signature for

_____ Arrow point credit

b. **Plant a tree in your yard, on the grounds of the group that operates your Cub Scout pack, or in a park or other public place. Be sure to get permission first.**

Trees make buildings more attractive and help them stay cooler in summer.

Planting Seedlings

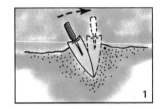

1. Push the trowel into the ground, and then push the handle up straight.

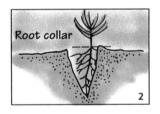

2. Remove the trowel and place the seedling with its root collar at ground level.

3. Push the trowel into the ground 2 inches from the seedling. Push the handle away from the plant. This will firm the soil at the bottom of the roots.

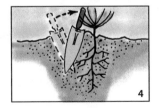

4. Now pull the handle toward the plant to firm the soil at the top of the roots.

5. Fill in the trowel hole by scraping the soil with your foot.

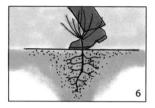

6. Pack the soil firmly around the seedling with your foot.

Some seedlings will be taller than you are in 5 years. You will be able to sit in their shade in 10 years.

_____ Bear credit

_____ /_____ Date and signature for

_____ Arrow point credit

---

c. Call city or county officials or your trash-hauling company and find out what happens to your trash after it is hauled away.

Is any of it

- Recycled?

- Burned to generate electricity?

If it is dumped and buried in a landfill, what will happen to the land afterward?

_____ Bear credit

_____ /_____ Date and signature for

_____ Arrow point credit

Achievements

> **d. Do a water-usage survey in your home. Note all the ways water is used. Look for any dripping faucets.**

_____ Cooking	_____ Garden
_____ Dish washing	_____ Shrubs and trees
_____ Laundry	_____ Swimming pool
_____ Showers and baths	_____ Drinking
_____ Toilets	_____ Fountains
_____ Lawn	_____ Hobbies

How to Repair a Leaky Faucet

1. With an adult, locate the shutoff valve for the faucet. Turn off the water.

2. Protect the finish of the packing nut by wrapping it with a soft cloth.

3. Loosen the packing nut carefully. Turn and lift out the stem assembly.

4. Remove the screw at the bottom of the stem assembly. Pry out the old washer. Clean out the place where it was.

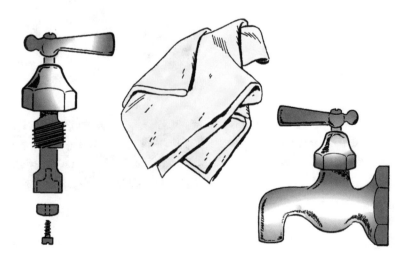

5. Replace the worn washer with one that fits. Insert flat side down. Replace the screw.

6. Wipe the valve seat clean. Replace the stem assembly. Wrap the soft cloth around the packing nut again, and then carefully tighten it. Turn on the valve. Test the faucet.

_____ / _____

_____ Bear credit

Date and signature for

_____ Arrow point credit

---

e. Discuss with an adult in your family the ways your family uses energy.

_____ Solar	_____ Diesel fuel
_____ Natural gas	_____ Electricity
_____ Propane	_____ Wood
_____ Gasoline	_____ Kerosene
_____ Heating oil	_____ Charcoal briquettes

_____ / _____

_____ Bear credit

Date and signature for

_____ Arrow point credit

Achievements

Visit or call your power company for help in completing this requirement. Ask how electricity is generated for your home.

Check off the appliances you have and underline the ones that use a lot of electricity:

_____	Toaster	_____	Air conditioning unit
_____	Stove	_____	Fan
_____	Microwave	_____	Water heater
_____	Refrigerator	_____	Dishwasher
_____	Heater	_____	Washing machine
_____	Radio	_____	Clothes dryer
_____	TV	_____	Hair dryer
_____	Clock	_____	Iron
_____	Computer		

_____ _____   _____ _____
    (Other)   (Other)

Achievements

To save electricity:

- Turn off lights when no one is using them.

- Turn off the TV when no one is watching.

- Turn the thermostat to 68° in winter and 78° in summer.

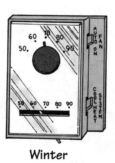 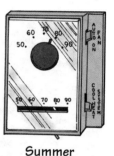

Summer

Winter

_____ / _____
_____ Bear credit
_____ Date and signature for
_____ Arrow point credit

CUB SCOUT LEADER BALOO SAYS:
When you have done three of these requirements, have a parent or an adult sign here.

_____ / _____ Date and signature for achievement 6

Enforcement Is a Big Job

Police officers need our help as they work to protect us. We need to understand ways of taking care of ourselves. Crime has always been a problem everywhere. But we can do something about it. This achievement will help you understand how the police and others fight crime. It will also show you ways that you can help.

REQUIREMENTS

Do four of the following requirements:

> ### a. Make a set of your own fingerprints.

Use an ink pad. Press your finger on the pad and then on a piece of paper. When you can get a good sharp print, make your set of prints right here in the book. Those prints are your signature. No one else on Earth has prints just like them.

Police look for fingerprints at the scene of a crime so that when they arrest someone, they can compare that person's prints against the ones found at the crime scene. If the prints match, it proves that the person had been there.

1. R. THUMB	2. R. INDEX	3. R. MIDDLE	4. R. RING	5. R. LITTLE
6. L. THUMB	7. L. INDEX	8. L. MIDDLE	9. L. RING	10. L. LITTLE

Achievements

_____ Bear credit

_____ /_____ Date and signature for

_____ Arrow point credit

b. Make a plaster cast of a shoeprint.

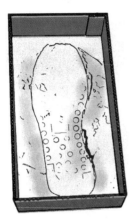

Make a good clear track in sand or soft earth. Put a cardboard ring around it. Mix water with plaster of paris until it's like thin pudding. Pour it over the track and let it harden.

Pick up the hardened plaster. Clean off any dirt that has stuck to it. Take off the shoe that made the track. Compare the sole of the shoe to the plaster shoeprint.

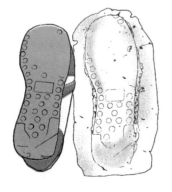

Police do this to find evidence that would tie a suspect to a crime scene. A shoeprint found at the crime scene that matches a suspect's shoe is an important piece of evidence.

_____ Bear credit
_____ / _____ Date and signature for
_____ Arrow point credit

Achievements

c. Check the doors and windows of your home.

Be sure you have tight, strong locks on your doors and windows. Do this with an adult in your family.

Place a board in the door frame to keep a sliding door from being forced open.

A deadbolt should be more than 1 inch long.

_____ Bear credit

_____ /_____ Date and signature for

_____ Arrow point credit

d. Visit your local sheriff's office or police station.

Meet the deputy sheriff or the police officer who patrols your neighborhood.

_____ Bear credit

_____ /_____ Date and signature for

_____ Arrow point credit

Achievements

e. Be sure you know where to get help in your neighborhood.

Is there a
- Block home?
- Emergency home?
- Helping-hand home?
- Family friend?

_____ Bear credit
_____ / _____ Date and signature for
_____ Arrow point credit

f. Be sure fire and police numbers are listed by the phone at your home.

Police_____

Fire _____

Check your phone book for emergency numbers. Memorize these numbers. See if you can dial or punch these numbers with your eyes closed.

_____ Bear credit
_____ / _____ Date and signature for
_____ Arrow point credit

g. Know what you can do to help law enforcement.

If you see a crime being committed or some dangerous activity, tell an adult or call the police.

Get the facts:
- What's happening?
- Where is it happening?
- Who is doing it?
  - —Can you describe the person?
  - —Did you get the license number?

WARNING

OPERATION I.D.
THIS PROPERTY PROTECTED

_____ / _____
_____ Bear credit
_____ Date and signature for
_____ Arrow point credit

CUB SCOUT LEADER BALOO SAYS:
When you have done four of these requirements, have a parent or an adult sign here.

_____ / _____
Date and signature for achievement 7

The Past Is Exciting and Important

Something that happened 100 years ago can seem as exciting and interesting as something that happened yesterday.

You learn about America's past in school. Your family has a history, too; so has your community and your Cub Scout pack.

REQUIREMENTS

Do three of the following requirements:

> **a. Visit your library or newspaper office. Ask to see back issues of newspapers or an almanac.**

What was happening in the world

- When you were born?

  _____

  _____

- On July 20, 1969?

  _____

  _____

- When you were 5 years old?

  _____

  _____

_____ Bear credit

_____ /_____ Date and signature for

_____ Arrow point credit

b. Find someone who was a Cub Scout a long time ago. Talk with him about what Cub Scouting was like then.

What did he do at

- Den meetings?

_____

_____

_____

- Pack meetings?

_____

_____

_____

What kind of uniform did he wear?

_____

_____

_____

_____ Bear credit
_____ / _____ Date and signature for
_____ Arrow point credit

c. Start or add to an existing pack scrapbook.

You might add a
- Picture
- Pack meeting program in which you took part
- Newspaper from your school
- Report on a Good Turn or service project done by your den or pack

_____ Bear credit
_____ / _____ Date and signature for
_____ Arrow point credit

d. Trace your family back through your grandparents or great-grandparents; or talk to a grandparent about what it was like when he or she was younger.

What did he or she do
- At school?
- During holidays?
- At home to help around the house?

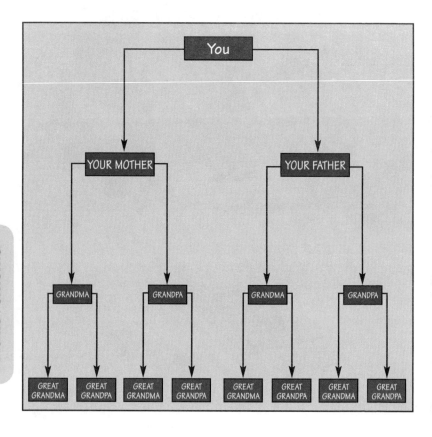

_____ Bear credit

_____ /_____ Date and signature for

_____ Arrow point credit

Achievements

e. Find out some history about your community.

Perhaps you can talk to someone who has lived in your community for a long time.

- How did people heat their homes?
- Where was the first school?
- Where was the fire station?
- Where were the places of worship?

You might find some books about the history of your community in your library.

_____ / _____

_____ Bear credit
_____ Date and signature for
_____ Arrow point credit

f. Write in a journal for 2 weeks.

Jot down some of the things you do each day. Be sure to keep your journal. When you grow up, you'll have some history about yourself.

_____ / _____

_____ Bear credit
_____ Date and signature for
_____ Arrow point credit

CUB SCOUT LEADER BALOO SAYS:
When you have done three requirements, have a parent or an adult sign here.

_____/_____ Date and signature for achievement 8

What's Cooking?

We all like to eat good things. Good things seem to taste even better when we make them ourselves. In this achievement you will want to work with someone who knows how to cook. You and that person can cook up some great food.

DO NOT TRY TO DO ANY OF THESE REQUIREMENTS UNLESS AN ADULT IS HELPING YOU!

Do four of the following requirements:

> **a. With an adult, bake cookies.**

How to Make Oatmeal Cookies

Preheat oven to 350°F.

¾ cup vegetable shortening
1 cup firmly packed brown sugar
½ cup granulated sugar
1 egg
¼ cup water
1 teaspoon vanilla
3 cups uncooked oats
1 cup all-purpose flour
1 teaspoon salt (optional)
½ teaspoon baking soda

Beat together the shortening, sugars, egg, water, and vanilla until creamy. Combine the remaining ingredients, add to the first mixture, and mix well. Drop by rounded teaspoonfuls onto a greased cookie sheet. Bake at 350°F for 12 to 15 minutes. For variety, add chopped nuts, raisins, chocolate chips, or coconut. Makes about 60 cookies.

If you don't like oatmeal cookies, use another recipe from a cookbook. Or use a packaged mix and follow the directions on the package.

Achievements

_____ Bear credit
_____ / _____ Date and signature for
_____ Arrow point credit

HARD-BOILED EGGS

Place eggs in a cooking pot or pan. Cover with cold water. Bring the water to a full boil. Reduce the heat and simmer for 15 minutes. Drain the hot water and replace it with cold. Drain and let the eggs dry. Put them in the refrigerator until you're ready to eat them. The egg is perfectly packaged by nature for picnics.

CARROT AND CELERY STICKS

Brush carrots and celery clean. Pare off dark spots. Cut off tops and bottoms. Cut in half lengthwise. Cut the half strips in quarters. Then cut into sticks.

POPCORN

Make some popcorn the "old-fashioned" way before there were hot air poppers and microwaves. Pour enough cooking oil into a large pan to cover the bottom. Add corn, spreading it so that each kernel is touching the bottom. Place the pan on medium-high heat and cover it with a tight-fitting lid. Gently shake the pan throughout popping so the corn won't burn. When the popping stops, remove the pan from the heat and pour the popcorn into a bowl. Add melted butter or margarine. Salt to taste.

_____ Bear credit

_____ / _____ Date and signature for

_____ Arrow point credit

Achievements

> **c. Prepare one part of your breakfast, one part of your lunch, and one part of your supper.**

JUICE
Squeeze fresh oranges, or you can use frozen orange juice or a mix. Follow the directions on the can or the package.

COOKED CEREAL
Follow the directions on the package.

SANDWICHES AND SOUP
This combination makes a good lunch any time of the year. Use canned soup or a mix. Follow the directions on the can or package. Make your sandwiches with whatever you have. Luncheon meat, cheese slices, sliced tomatoes, lettuce, and mayonnaise make a super sandwich. You don't need to have all of that in one sandwich. You could make three different kinds. Peanut butter and jelly also make a good sandwich.

Spread peanut butter on one slice of bread and jelly on the other. Put the two together and slice in half. Replace the jar covers and clean the spreading knife.

BOILED POTATOES

Use a potato peeler to peel enough potatoes for your family. (One for each person is about right.) Wash the potatoes and cut them in quarters. Put the potatoes in a pan and add enough water to cover them. Add ¼ teaspoon of salt. Cover the pan. Bring the water to a boil, and then reduce the heat. Cook for 20 minutes or until you can easily push a fork into a potato. Remove from the heat. Drain the water, using the cover to keep the potatoes from spilling out. Replace on the heat for about 10 seconds to dry. Serve with butter, margarine, or gravy.

BOILED CARROTS

Carrots can be cooked the same way as potatoes.

SPAGHETTI

Follow the directions on the package.

_____ Bear credit
_____ /_____ Date and signature for
_____ Arrow point credit

d. Make a list of the "junk" foods you eat. Discuss "junk" food with a parent or teacher.

Junk foods have too many calories and too few nutrients. Foods with a lot of sugar might not have the vitamins and minerals you need.

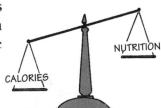

- Soft drinks
- Candy
- Ice cream
- Chips

_____ / _____Teacher's signature

_____ Bear credit

_____ / _____ Date and signature for

_____ Arrow point credit

NUTS AND BOLTS

Mix peanuts and raisins together with some dry cereal.

_____ Bear credit

_____ / _____ Date and signature for

_____ Arrow point credit

f. Make a dessert for your family.

INSTANT PUDDING
Empty the contents of the package into a bowl. Follow the directions on the package.

BROWNIES
Follow the directions on the package.

FLAVORED GELATIN
Follow the directions on the package.

_____ Bear credit
_____ /_____ Date and signature for
_____ Arrow point credit

CUB SCOUT LEADER BALOO SAYS:
When you have done four of these requirements, have a parent or an adult sign here.

_____ /_____ Date and signature for achievement 9

Family Fun

A family is people who live together and take care of each other. Get to know your family better by spending more time with them.

Plan a trip or a fun evening together. Talk about your plans. A parent or guardian is like Baloo, a Cub Scout leader who can show you many useful and interesting things.

REQUIREMENTS

Do both of these requirements:

---

a. Go on a trip with members of your family.

Visit one of the following:

_____ Park   _____ Museum
_____ Airport   _____ Seashore
_____ Farm or ranch

BEFORE YOU GO. Think of the things that you might need, and pack them in a handy bag. Your needs might differ according to how you are traveling (by car, train, bus, subway, ferry, or bicycle or on foot).

CAR BEHAVIOR AND SAFETY. An adult family member should make sure the car is safe to drive before the trip begins.

You will be expected to get yourself ready and agree to

- Buckle yourself in with a seat belt. Urge others use theirs; in many states, it's the law. Make sure infants and small children ride in safe car seats or child restraints.
- Change seats only at roadside stops. Don't climb from one seat to another while the car is moving.
- Keep your hands and arms inside the car.
- Keep doors locked at all times.
- Keep the rear window of a station wagon closed.
- Save paper and trash for roadside barrels. Don't litter.
- Pack everything in the trunk or carrier except snacks, game bag, and books.
- Don't be noisy or shout inside the car.
- Use good manners and be considerate of others while traveling on a bus, train, subway, ferry, or other public means of transportation.

Achievements

WHAT TO DO FOR A TRIP IN TOWN

Find out what time tours are given at a museum or other place of interest. Ask if a reservation is required. Arrive on time. Stay with your group. Treat your guide with respect. Listen to what he or she says. Keep the noise down—be polite.

_____ Bear credit

_____ /_____ Date and signature for

_____ Arrow point credit

b. Have a family "make-and-do" night.

Get together and make homemade games, things for the holidays, or party decorations.

STADIUM SEAT

Place rug or foam rubber scraps between two pieces of carpeting. Lay a rope handle in place, cement, and sew around the edges.

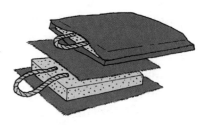

BOOT JACK

Make it easy to take off yo[ur] boots or overshoes. Any piece of 1-inch-thick scrap wood that is 1 foot long and 3 inches wide will do. Cut a V in one end. Then nail a short piece of wood beneath the point of the V.

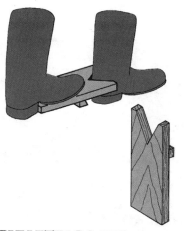

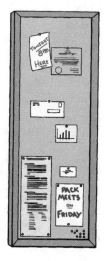

BULLETIN BOARD

A long narrow bulletin board is easy for all members of the family to read. Put the grown-ups' notices at the top and the children's at the bottom. Start with a panel from a corrugated box. Cover it with plain cloth. Tack it to a narrow wooden frame.

_____ Bear credit

_____ / _____ Date and signature for

_____ Arrow point credit

CUB SCOUT LEADER BALOO SAYS:
When you have completed both requirements, have a parent or an adult sign here.

_____ / _____ Date and signature for achievement 10

...dy

You can expect firefighters, police officers, and paramedics to help and protect you in an emergency. Sometimes, though, you have to take care of yourself or someone else until help arrives. You should be ready to do the right thing if this happens.

Fires and accidents can be frightening, and it is natural to be scared. That is why we think about what to do before an emergency happens.

In a very serious case, there is little time to stop and figure out what to do. That is why we must be ready. If someone's clothes are on fire, or breathing has stopped, you must act at once. In other emergencies there might be time to stop a few seconds and think about what to do.

Your best way to handle most emergencies is to get help from an adult.

A good way to be ready is to carry enough change for a pay phone. Some pay phones don't require money to reach an operator—you just press "0." In some areas you can dial 911 for help. Find out if you can do that where you live.

REQUIREMENTS

Do the first four requirements; the last one is recommended, but not required.

> **a. Tell what to do in case of an accident in the home. A family member needs help. Someone's clothes catch on fire.**

What should you do if you are at home with a family member and he or she falls down the stairs or off of a ladder and gets hurt? Talk it over with an adult and think about these things:

1. Be calm and make the person as comfortable as possible without moving him or her. Don't try to move an injured person. You might make the injury worse if you do.

2. GET HELP! If there is someone in the yard or nearby, send that person to get a neighbor or call for an ambulance. Do it yourself if no one else is around.

3. Stay with the injured person. Use a blanket to keep him or her warm.

What should you do if someone's clothes catch on fire? Find out. Talk it over with an adult.

1. Usually a person panics and starts to run—stop him! Running fans the flames and makes them spread.

2. If the person can be caught, force him or her to the ground or floor. Roll the victim over and over to smother the flames. Wrap them with a rug, blanket, or sweater, working from the neck down. If you can't catch the victim, yell "Stop! Stop! Stop!," and then throw yourself on the ground and roll so the victim can see you and do what you do. **Cover your face.**

3. As soon as you can, help the person get to a place where the burned parts of the body can be covered with clean dressings and treated by a doctor.

Achievements

What should you do if your own clothes catch on fire?

1. **Stop** where you are. **Don't run!**
2. Drop to the floor or ground.
3. Roll and cover your face.
4. If you are indoors, grab a rug, blanket, or coat and wrap yourself as you roll. Start at your neck.

What should you do if your house catches on fire?

1. First, get everyone out of the house! Crawl along the floor to avoid breathing smoke.
2. Don't try to put the fire out yourself.
3. Call the fire department from a neighbor's house.
4. When the firefighters arrive, let them know everyone is out of the house.

Remember: Never go back into a burning building for any reason.

_____ Bear credit
_____ / _____ Date and signature for
_____ Arrow point credit

b. Tell what to do in case of a water accident.

A boat overturns and you are in it. What do you do?

1. **Don't panic.** Grab the boat and stay with it.

2. Help the other passengers to find a place where they can hold on. **No one should try to swim ashore.** Stay with the boat; it will support you. Wait for rescuers.

3. If the boat can be turned right side up, get inside and sit as low as possible on the bottom.

Someone slips off a bank into the water. What do you do?

Achievements

1. Reach the person, if possible, with your hand or leg. Take off your sweater or shirt and toss one end to the person. You can also extend a stick, fishing pole, branch, or anything that is handy.

2. Throw something to the person that will float, such as a cushion, inner tube, plank, or a ring buoy, if available.

Someone falls through the ice. What do you do?

1. Remember, if you get too close, you might break through, too.

2. Find something to throw to the person.

3. Look around for a ladder, a long branch, or anything you can use to reach toward the person. Lie flat on safe ice and push the item toward the person until he or she can grab it. Then you can pull him or her out.

4. When the person is out of the water, get him or her to someplace warm.

_____ Bear credit

_____ /_____ Date and signature for

_____ Arrow point credit

c. Tell what to do in case of a school bus accident.

1. Always know where emergency exits are whenever you get on a bus.

2. In case of an accident, follow directions from the driver. If the driver is injured, stay calm. Tell others to take it easy and get out of the bus through the emergency exits. Move to the side of the road, away from traffic.

3. Help the bus driver get everyone out without pushing.

_____ Bear credit

_____ / _____ Date and signature for

_____ Arrow point credit

d. Tell what to do in case of a car accident.

1. Be calm. Help the adults by doing what you are told.

2. Suggest to the driver that the car be left where it is until the police come. Ask an adult to direct traffic around it.

3. Don't go out into the road yourself. Watch for other cars. All passengers should get out of the car on the side away from traffic.

4. **Don't move anyone who might be badly injured.**

_____ Bear credit
_____ / _____ Date and signature for
_____ Arrow point credit

---

e. Have a health checkup by a physician (optional).

RECOMMENDED, BUT NOT REQUIRED. A health checkup is a good thing to have each year. It will show you what to do for your health's sake.

_____ Bear credit
_____ / _____ Date and signature for
_____ Arrow point credit

CUB SCOUT LEADER BALOO SAYS:
When you have done the first four requirements—the last requirement is recommended, but not required— have a parent or an adult sign here.

_____/_____ Date and signature for
achievement 11

Family Outdoor Adventures

You might live in a state that has snow in winter, or you might live where it is warm all the time. No matter where you live, being outside and doing things with your family is great. You can have fun together and get to know one another better.

REQUIREMENTS

Do three of the following requirements:

> ### a. Go camping with your family.

CAMPING

When you spend time outdoors and stay overnight in a tent, camper, trailer, or motor home, that's camping. Be sure to help your family pack for the trip. You will need to be ready for changes in the weather. It can get cold at night or rain suddenly. Pack things that keep you warm and dry.

_____ / _____

_____ Bear credit
_____ Date and signature for
_____ Arrow point credit

> ### b. Go on a hike with your family.

HIKING

A hike is more than a walk. When you hike, you go exploring to find out something. You can hike in the city; forest preserves; county, state, or national parks; or even the zoo. **Never hike alone.**

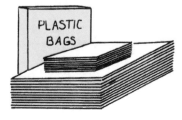

KEEPING DRY

When you are far from shelter, what will you do when it rains? Some smart outdoor families have solved that problem. Each family member carries a plastic

30 GALLON TRASH BAG PONCHO

1 GALLON FOOD STORAGE BAG RAIN HAT

CUT

CUT

trash-bag poncho. When it rains, just slip it over your head and wear it like a sleeveless sweater. You can also make a rain cap from a plastic food-storage bag.

Keep away from hilltops and trees that could draw lightning.

SUN SAFETY

Too much sun can be dangerous. Follow these tips from the American Academy of Dermatology to stay safe in the sun:

- Try to stay out of the sun between 10 A.M. and 4 P.M. when the sun's rays are the strongest.

- Use lots of sunscreen with a sun protection factor (SPF) of at least 15. Put on more every two hours when you're outdoors, even on cloudy days.

- Wear protective, tightly woven clothing, such as a long-sleeved shirt and pants.

- Wear a 4-inch-wide broad-brimmed hat and sunglasses with lenses that protect you against the sun's ultraviolet rays (called UV protection).

- Stay in the shade whenever you can.

- Stay away from reflective surfaces, which can reflect up to 85 percent of the sun's damaging rays.

DON'T GET LOST!

Stay with your family. Don't wander off by yourself. Carry a police whistle to signal for help if you get lost. Three sharp blasts on your whistle means "Emergency!"

LEAVE YOUR TRACKS.

Even with careful planning and with clear instructions to follow the buddy plan, sometimes a hiker can become separated from the group. When hikers are lost, searchers need to know what their tracks look like. Before setting out on a hike into the woods, have the hikers in your group leave their tracks. Here's how to leave your tracks: Fold a soft towel until it is roughly the size of your hiking shoe. Place the folded towel on a newspaper and cover it with a piece of aluminum foil. Stand on the foil and step off. The print you make can help searchers find you if necessary. Write the color of your clothes on a slip of paper and leave it with your footprint.

Tell someone where your group is going and when you will return. Give that person the aluminum foil tracks of all the hik-

ing shoes. If someone gets separated from the group or if the group doesn't get back on time, that person can alert the authorities and give them the information they need for their search.

STAY WHERE YOU ARE.

If you ever think you are lost, sit down and wait in the open where people can see you. Searchers will find you. **Don't try to find your way back.**

_____ / _____

_____ Bear credit
_____ Date and signature for
_____ Arrow point credit

c. Have a picnic with your family.

How about a breakfast picnic?

How about an all-star favorite-food roundup? That's when everyone brings his or her favorite food to share with others.

_____ Bear credit

_____ / _____ Date and signature for

_____ Arrow point credit

d. Attend an outdoor event with your family.

A craft fair

A hot-air balloon race

A bird count

A fish derby

_____ Bear credit
_____ /_____ Date and signature for
_____ Arrow point credit

e. Plan your outdoor family day.

Think of some things you would like to do outdoors. Explain these ideas to your family. Listen carefully to the ideas other family members have.

_____ Bear credit
_____ /_____ Date and signature for
_____ Arrow point credit

Achievements

CUB SCOUT LEADER BALOO SAYS:
When you have done three of these requirements, have a parent or an adult sign here.

_____ /_____ Date and signature for
achievement 12

Achievement 13

People can do a lot of things with money. They can buy or build a house. Cars, clothes, food—almost everything we need or use takes money. We can make some things. We can raise or grow some foods. When we do that we save money.

You might have an allowance, or you might earn money for the things you need each week. Money is going to be important to you all of your life. Now is a good time to learn how to manage it.

REQUIREMENTS

Do four of the following requirements:

> **a. Go grocery shopping with a parent or other adult member of your family.**

Compare the prices of different brands of the same item. Check the prices at different stores.

Read the ads in your newspaper.

_____ / _____
_____ Bear credit
Date and signature for
_____ Arrow point credit

> **b. Set up a savings account.**

When you put your money in a bank or savings and loan institution, the bank puts your money to work for you. The bank loans your money to people who need it, charging a fee (called *interest*) to the borrower for the use of your money. This interest is then added to your account. You may withdraw your money whenever you need it.

A savings account helps you save your money. The interest adds to the balance, and you may add more money as it becomes available to you. This makes it easier for you to save money for something special.

_____ / _____
_____ Bear credit
Date and signature for
_____ Arrow point credit

Achievements

c. Keep a record of how you spend money for 2 weeks.

Date	How I Spent Money	How Much I Spent

When you have finished the record, look over each line. Did you spend that money wisely? Did you buy some things you didn't need? What can you do to manage your money better from now on?

_______ Bear credit

__________ /__________________________ Date and signature for

_______ Arrow point credit

Achievements

d. Pretend you are shopping for a car for your family.

Look through car ads in the newspaper. Compare the prices of cars. Are the cars large enough for your family? How about miles per gallon? Pick one that you think is best for your family. Report your choice to your parent or guardian. Tell why you picked that car.

Achievements

e. Discuss family finances with a parent or guardian.

Find out how you can help with family finances.

_____ Bear credit
_____ /_____ Date and signature for
_____ Arrow point credit

f. Play a board game with your family that involves the use of play money.

Does the person who wins most of the time take fewer chances? Or more chances? Are you getting better at the game?

_____ Bear credit
_____ /_____ Date and signature for
_____ Arrow point credit

Achievements

g. With an adult, figure out how much it costs for each person in your home to eat one meal.

Before the meal is prepared, jot down the cost of each of the foods used.

COST PER MEAL

PEOPLE	FOOD COST

Divide the total cost of the food by the number of people who will be eating the meal.

Is this more or less than what it would cost to eat out?

_____ Bear credit
_____ /_____ Date and signature for
_____ Arrow point credit

CUB SCOUT LEADER BALOO SAYS:
When you have done four of the requirements, have a parent or an adult sign here.

_____ /_____ Date and signature for
achievement 13

Right

Bicycle motocross (BMX), road bikes and mountain bikes, bike hikes—there are all kinds of bicycles and things to do with them today. Boys and girls and grown-ups, too, are riding bikes more and more.

Bicycling is fun, it's good for you, and it's interesting. But bicycling can be dangerous if you are not careful. Be sure you know the safety rules for bicycling, and be sure you and your family always keep your bikes in good shape.

Here are the requirements to complete your Ride Right achievement.

Achievement 14 (side margin)

REQUIREMENTS

Do requirement *a* and three more of the other six requirements.

> **a. Know the rules for bike safety. If your town requires a bicycle license, be sure to get one.**

Rules for Bike Safety

1. Obey all traffic signs and signals.
2. Ride single file on streets and highways and keep to the right, with the flow of traffic.
3. Ride in a straight line. Don't do stunts or weave in and out of traffic.
4. Use proper hand signals when in traffic.

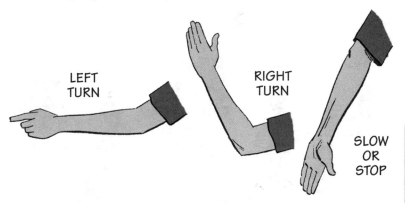

LEFT TURN

RIGHT TURN

SLOW OR STOP

5. Slow down and look carefully before you cross any intersection.
6. Be alert for other vehicles, especially for cars pulling out from the curb.
7. Don't shoot out of blind alleys and driveways.
8. Give pedestrians the right-of-way.
9. Don't carry another rider.
10. Don't hitch onto cars and trucks.

a. Continued

11. Be sure your bike has good brakes and a warning bell or horn.
12. If you must ride at night, be sure to have a headlight on the front of your bike and a red reflector on the rear.
13. Always wear a helmet.

10/11/01 / _____

_____ ✓ Bear credit
_____ Date and signature for
_____ Arrow point credit

---

b. Learn to ride a bike, if you haven't by now. Show that you can follow a winding course for 60 feet doing sharp left and right turns, a U-turn, and an emergency stop.

Note: Using a Snell- or ANSI-approved bike helmet is recommended.

10/11/01 / _____

_____ ✓ Bear credit
_____ Date and signature for
_____ Arrow point credit

c. Keep your bike in good shape. Identify the parts of a bike that should be checked often.

✓ Brakes	✓ Chain
✓ Spokes	✓ Tires
✓ Pedals	✓ Reflectors
✓ Seat	✓ Lights

Which of these parts should be repaired by an expert only?

Explain and show how you protect your bike from bad weather. Always keep your bike under shelter when it is not in use. If it gets wet from rain or snow, wipe it dry. Keep the moving parts well lubricated. Have someone help you learn how to work with any parts that need adjusting.

10/11/01

_____ Bear credit
Date and signature for
_____ Arrow point credit

d. Change a tire on a bicycle.

1.

Scrape the tube over the hole.

2.

Apply cement. Rub it in with your finger and let it dry.

3.

Remove the cover from the patch.

4.

Apply the patch with pressure.

5.

Put a little air in the tube. Insert the tube into the tire and place it on the rim. Finish filling the tube with air. Check the air pressure.

_____ Bear credit

_____ / _____ Date and signature for

_____ Arrow point credit

e. Protect your bike from theft. Use a bicycle lock.

Write down your bicycle's serial number and keep it in a safe place. Have your name engraved somewhere on your bike.

_____ Bear credit

_____ / _____ Date and signature for

_____ Arrow point credit

f. Ride a bike for 1 mile without rest. Be sure to obey all traffic rules.

10/11/01, RJW99

_____ ✓ Bear credit
Date and signature for
_____ Arrow point credit

g. Plan and take a family bike hike.

_____ Bear credit
_____ /_____ Date and signature for
_____ Arrow point credit

CUB SCOUT LEADER BALOO SAYS:
When you have done requirement
a and three others, have a parent
or an adult sign here.

_____ /_____ Date and signature for
achievement 14

Games, Games, Games!

Let's play a game! Everybody likes games, especially outdoor games. Here are some game ideas. You might have played some of them, but you will probably find new ones. Games are fun and they teach you how to think before you act.

REQUIREMENTS

Do two of the following requirements:

a. Set up the equipment and play any two of these outdoor games with your family or friends.

_____ Backyard golf   _____ Kickball
_____ Badminton   _____ Softball
_____ Croquet   _____ Tetherball
_____ Sidewalk   _____ Horseshoes
      shuffleboard   _____ Volleyball

NOTE for Akela: Also see badminton, softball, and volleyball in the *Cub Scout Academics and Sports Program Guide.*

_____ Bear credit

_____ /_____ Date and signature for

_____ Arrow point credit

b. Play two organized games with your den.

Pick games that everyone can play.

_____ Bear credit

_____ / _____ Date and signature for

_____ Arrow point credit

c. Select a game that your den has never played. Explain the rules. Tell them how to play it, and then play it with them.

Did they understand your explanation? Do you think they will want to play it again?

_____ / _____
_____ Bear credit
_____ Date and signature for
_____ Arrow point credit

CUB SCOUT LEADER BALOO SAYS:
When you have done two requirements, have a parent or an adult sign here.

_____ / _____
Date and signature for achievement 15

Building Muscles

Games, stunts, and contests with other Cub Scouts help you become physically fit and alert. Den and pack activities are aimed at keeping you healthy.

This achievement will develop your speed, balance, and reactions. The more you practice, the stronger you will become. A strong body is important to you now, and it will be even more important to you as you grow older.

REQUIREMENTS

Do all of the following requirements:

> **a. Do physical fitness stretching exercises. Then do curl-ups, push-ups, the standing long jump, and the softball throw.**

Stretching exercises

Curl-ups

Standing long jump

Push-ups

Softball throw

_____ Bear credit
_____ /_____ Date and signature for
_____ Arrow point credit

_____ **ONE-PERSON PUSH OVER LINE.** Face your opponent. Grasp his shoulders. On the word "Go," try to push him across the line. Your goal line is 10 feet in front of you; your opponent's is 10 feet behind you. Only pushing is permitted.

_____ **PULL OVER.** Indicate a circle on the ground, 15 or 20 feet across. Stand back-to-back, lean forward, place your hands on the floor. Now grab your opponent's right hand between your legs. On the signal "Go," try to pull your friend out of his half of the circle.

_____ **ONE-PERSON PULL OVER LINE.** Face your friend 3 feet away from him. Grasp his wrists and try to pull him across the goal line 10 feet behind you. Only pulling is allowed.

_____ Bear credit
_____ /_____ Date and signature for
_____ Arrow point credit

FOOT PUSH. Sit facing your friend. Have the soles of your feet touching with your knees bent. Try to push your friend out of a circle or over a line. Feet must always be touching feet. Push on the floor with your hands.

ONE-LEGGED HAND WRESTLE. Hold your left ankle with your left hand. Take your friend's right hand. On the word "Go," try to get him to let go of his foot or lose his balance.

STAND UP BACK-TO-BACK PUSH. Stand back-to-back with your elbows linked. Try to push your friend across a line 10 feet away. Only pushing is allowed.

SEATED BACK-TO-BACK PUSH. Sit back-to-back. Fold your arms across your chest. Using your feet on the floor, try to push your friend over a line. Don't push or butt with your head!

_____ Bear credit

_____ / _____ Date and signature for

_____ Arrow point credit

_____ **HAND WRESTLE.** Grasp your friend's right hand. Stand with the outside of your right foot braced against his. Spread your feet so that you are well balanced. On the signal "Go," try to throw your friend off balance. The first player to move a foot or touch the ground with a hand is the loser.

_____ **ELBOW WRESTLE.** Lie on your stomach, facing your friend (who is lying on his stomach). Place your right elbow on the floor and clasp your friend's right hand. Try to force his hand to the floor at the command "Go." Elbows must not leave the floor. Try it with left hands.

_____ Bear credit

_____ / _____ Date and signature for

_____ Arrow point credit

c. Compete with your den or pack in the crab relay, gorilla relay, 30-yard dash, and kangaroo relay.

CRAB RELAY

Achievements

30-YARD DASH

GORILLA RELAY

KANGAROO RELAY

_____ Bear credit
_____ / _____ Date and signature for
_____ Arrow point credit

NOTE TO PARENTS: If a licensed physician certifies that the Cub Scout's physical condition for an indeterminable time doesn't permit him to do three of the requirements in this achievement, the Cubmaster and the pack committee may authorize substitution of any three Arrow Point electives.

CUB SCOUT LEADER BALOO SAYS:
When you have done all three requirements, have a parent or an adult sign here.

_____ / _____ Date and signature for
achievement 16

Information, Please

Information is a big word with a simple meaning. It means *facts*, and telling someone a fact is communication. We can also get information from newspapers, books, magazines, radio, TV, and computers.

As you complete this achievement, you might be surprised to find out all of the ways we can give and get information.

REQUIREMENTS

Do requirement *a* and three more of the following requirements:

> **a. With an adult in your family, choose a TV show. Watch it together.**

After the show, talk about it.
- What did you like?
- What did you learn?
- What didn't you like?
- What would you have changed?

_____ / _____
_____ Bear credit
Date and signature for
_____ Arrow point credit

> **b. Play a game of charades at your den meeting or with your family at home.**

Charades is a guessing game. During the game, you give information without talking, and your friends guess what you mean. Each part of a word is acted out. Suppose the word is "football." You might point to your foot. When your team yells "foot," you could pretend to kick a ball. Don't use your voice at all during this game.

_____ / _____
_____ Bear credit
Date and signature for
_____ Arrow point credit

Achievements

c. Visit a newspaper office or a TV or radio station and talk to a news reporter.

- Where does the reporter get the news?
- How does the reporter put the story together?
- Where does the story go after the reporter finishes it?

_____ Bear credit
_____ / _____ Date and signature for
_____ Arrow point credit

d. Use a computer to get information. Write, spell-check, and print out a report on what you learned.

Most computers are used to store or get information. If you have a computer at home, ask a parent or other adult family member to show you some of the information that it can help you find.

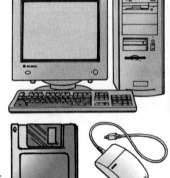

Computers are a part of our daily lives. They are a source of information, games, and messages. They are also a lot of fun.

Software companies have different programs with various formats. Be sure the one you are going to use will work with your brand of computer.

Pictures that appear on your computer screen are called *graphics*. They can be used to make story illustrations, games, certificates, and many other useful things.

_____ Bear credit
_____ / _____ Date and signature for
_____ Arrow point credit

Achievements

> **e. Write a letter to a company that makes something you use. Use e-mail or the U.S. Postal Service.**

Tell them what you like about their product. Ask them if they offer company tours, free samples, or catalogs.

_____ /_____

_____ Bear credit
Date and signature for
_____ Arrow point credit

> **f. Talk with a parent or other family member about how getting and giving facts fits into his or her job.**

How do they get the facts they need?
- Does someone tell them directly, or over the phone?
- Do they read it on paper, in books, or from a computer screen?
- What do they do with the facts?
- Do they pass the facts along to others?

_____ /_____

_____ Bear credit
Date and signature for
_____ Arrow point credit

Achievements

CUB SCOUT LEADER BALOO SAYS:
When you have done requirement *a* and three others, have a parent or an adult sign here.

_____/_____ Date and signature for
achievement 17

Jot It Down

Writing is one of the most important things humankind has learned to do. Writing lets us send messages to faraway places, make a lasting record of things we want to remember, and read what others have done or thought in the past. Being able to write clearly is a useful and satisfying skill. Do this achievement to learn more about it.

REQUIREMENTS

Do five of the following requirements:

---

a. Make a list of the things you want to do today. Check them off when you have done them.

Before you go to bed, make a list of the things you should do tomorrow. Put the list on the bulletin board or someplace where you will see it often so you won't forget anything.

_____ / _____

_____ Bear credit
_____ Date and signature for
_____ Arrow point credit

---

b. Write two letters to relatives or friends.

Tell them what you have been doing in Cub Scouting.

_____ / _____

_____ Bear credit
_____ Date and signature for
_____ Arrow point credit

c. Keep a daily record of your activities for 2 weeks.

Time yourself. When do you: TIME

    Get up in the morning?   _____

    Eat breakfast?   _____

    Go to school?   _____

    Eat lunch?   _____

    Get home from school?   _____

    Eat supper?   _____

    Do homework?   _____

    Watch TV?   _____

    Go to bed?   _____

Time yourself like this for 3 or 4 days. For the rest of the days, write what you did in the mornings, afternoons, and evenings.

_____ Bear credit

_____ /_____ Date and signature for

_____ Arrow point credit

Do you know a boy who could be a Cub Scout? Invite him to your den meeting.

Has your teacher ever come to a pack meeting? Send your teacher an invitation to your next pack meeting. Make your teacher an honorary member of your den.

Do you know what RSVP on an invitation means? It stands for words in the French language that mean "Please reply."

_____ Bear credit
_____ / _____ Date and signature for
_____ Arrow point credit

e. Write a story about something you have done with your family.

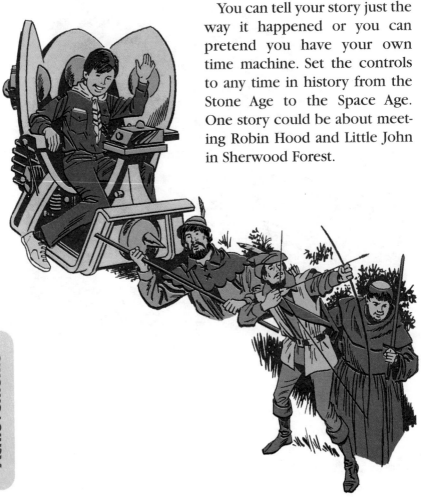

You can tell your story just the way it happened or you can pretend you have your own time machine. Set the controls to any time in history from the Stone Age to the Space Age. One story could be about meeting Robin Hood and Little John in Sherwood Forest.

_____ Bear credit

_____ /_____ Date and signature for

_____ Arrow point credit

f. Write a thank-you note.

When someone gives you a present, it's time to write a thank-you note. There are other times, too, such as when someone invites you to eat dinner, to see a movie, or to go swimming with them.

A thank-you note is always appreciated.

_____ / _____

_____ Bear credit
Date and signature for
_____ Arrow point credit

g. Write about the activities in your den.

Your pack might have its own newspaper, and its editor would like to have your story for the paper. If there isn't a pack paper, post your story on the bulletin board.

_____ / _____

_____ Bear credit
Date and signature for
_____ Arrow point credit

Achievements

CUB SCOUT LEADER BALOO SAYS:
When you have done five of the requirements, have a parent or an adult sign here.

_____/_____ Date and signature for achievement 18

Shavings and Chips

Your Cub Scout knife is an important tool. You can do many things with its blades. The cutting blade is the one you will use most of the time. With it you can make shavings and chips and carve all kinds of things.

You must be very careful and alert when you whittle or carve. Take good care of your knife. Always remember that a knife is a tool, not a toy. Use it with care so that you don't hurt yourself or ruin what you are carving.

Do all of the following requirements:

---

a. **Know the safety rules for handling a knife.**

Safety Rules

- A knife is a tool, not a toy.
- Know how to sharpen a knife. A sharp knife is safer because it is less likely to slip and cut you.
- Keep the blade clean.
- Never carry an open knife in your hand.
- When you are not using your knife, close it and put it away.
- Keep your knife dry.
- When you are using the cutting blade, do not try to make big shavings or chips. Easy does it.
- Make a safety circle: Before you pick up your knife to use it, stretch your arm out and turn in a circle. If you can't touch anyone else, it is safe to use your knife.

_____ Bear credit
_____ / _____ _____ Date and signature for
_____ Arrow point credit

---

b. **Show that you know how to take care of and use a pocketknife.**

SHARPENING A KNIFE.
Lay the blade on a sharpening stone as though you were going to shave a thin sliver from the stone. Push the blade forward. Turn the blade over and shave the

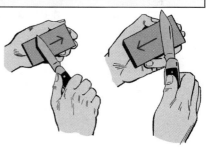

stone toward you. It is not necessary to push down hard. Continue this back-and-forth action until the edge is sharp along its whole length.

Achievements

SHARPENING STICK

If you don't have a sharpening stone, you can use a sharpening stick. Look at the picture to see how to make one. Cover a stick with a piece of inner tube. Tack it down. Cover the inner tube with emery cloth and tack it down as shown.

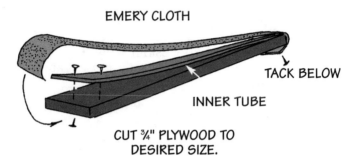

EMERY CLOTH

TACK BELOW

INNER TUBE

CUT ¾" PLYWOOD TO DESIRED SIZE.

SHAVINGS AND CHIPS

You don't have to be strong to whittle and carve, but you do have to be smart. Take it easy. Make a lot of small shavings and cuts. Here is the secret: Before you make a shaving cut, make a stop cut. At the place you want the shaving to stop, cut straight down with your knife. Press down and rock the blade back and forth until the cut is as deep as you want the shaving to go. Then make the shaving cut into it and lift away the shaving.

SHAVING CUT

STOP CUT

_____ Bear credit

_____ / _____ Date and signature for

_____ Arrow point credit

Achievements

c. Make a carving with a pocketknife. Work with your den leader or other adult when doing this.

TRACE THE PATTERN.

Eskimos carve beautiful animals from walrus ivory. They make seals, bears, dogs, and people. You can make a carving of a bear that looks like an Eskimo carving. Carve it out of soap.

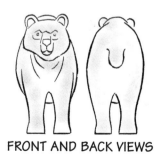

MAKE BOTH SIDES THE SAME.

FRONT AND BACK VIEWS

_____ Bear credit
_____ /_____ Date and signature for
_____ Arrow point credit

Achievements

Knives Are Not Toys

- Close the blade with the palm of your hand.
- Never use a knife on something that will dull or break it.
- Be careful that you do not cut yourself or any person nearby.
- Never use a knife to strip the bark from a tree.
- Do not carve your initials into anything that does not belong to you.

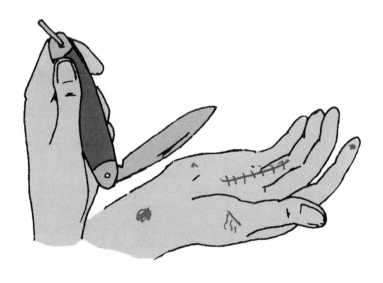

_____ Bear credit

_____ / _____ Date and signature for

_____ Arrow point credit

Achievements

Pocketknife Pledge

- I understand the reason for safety rules.
- I will treat my pocketknife with the respect due a useful tool.
- I will always close my pocketknife and put it away when I'm not using it.
- I will not use my pocketknife when it might injure someone near me.
- I promise never to throw my pocketknife for any reason.
- I will use my pocketknife in a safe manner at all times.

_____ Bear credit

_____ / _____ Date and signature for

_____ Arrow point credit

CUB SCOUT LEADER BALOO SAYS:
When you have done all the requirements, have a parent or an adult sign here.

_____ / _____ Date and signature for achievement 19

...ust and Nails

When you can cut wood to the right length and fasten it together with nails, you're a handyman, but there are more tools than just a hammer and saw. You will need something to hold the wood in place while you work on it. Sometimes you will need to make a curved cut or put a hole through the wood.

A good way to learn how to use tools is to watch someone using them. When you need to make something with wood, ask your parent or another adult to show you how to use the tools safely.

WARNING: DO NOT USE ELECTRICAL TOOLS UNLESS AN ADULT HELPS YOU.

REQUIREMENTS

Do all of the following requirements:

> **a. Show how to use and take care of four of these tools.**

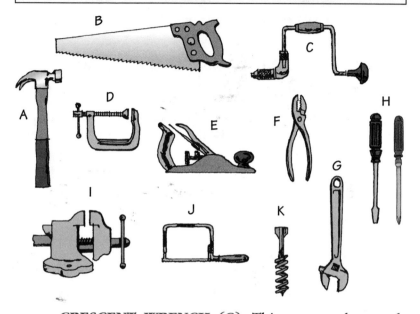

_____ **CRESCENT WRENCH (G).** This open-end wrench can be adjusted to fit many sizes of nuts.

_____ **COPING SAW (J).** Lets you cut curves.

_____ **C-CLAMP (D).** Holds pieces of wood together after gluing.

_____ **HAND SAW (B).** There are two kinds: one for cross-cutting, and another for ripping lengthwise along the grain of the wood.

_____ **DRILL BIT (K).** Corkscrew-shaped drills are called drill bits. They are used to drill holes in wood.

_____ **HAMMER (A).** Used for driving nails, for prying boards apart, and for pulling nails.

Achievements

_____ **HAND DRILL (C).** Uses drill bits to bore holes in wood and metal.

_____ **BENCH VISE (I).** Holds wood in place for sawing or planing.

_____ **WOOD PLANE (E).** Smooths rough boards.

_____ **SCREWDRIVER (H).** Sets screws.

_____ **PLIERS (F).** Slip-joint pliers have wide and normal jaw openings to grip things of different sizes. (Don't use pliers on nuts—use a crescent wrench instead.)

_____ Bear credit

_____ /_____ Date and signature for

_____ Arrow point credit

b. Build your own toolbox.

You will need three 1-by-6-inch pieces of wood. The two side pieces are 20 inches long. The bottom piece is 18½ inches long.

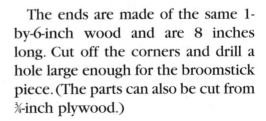

THE HANDLE IS A BROOM-STICK PIECE OR DOWEL.

20"

1"

6"

The ends are made of the same 1-by-6-inch wood and are 8 inches long. Cut off the corners and drill a hole large enough for the broomstick piece. (The parts can also be cut from ¾-inch plywood.)

Achievements

Did you know that wood sizes are measured when boards are still rough? When the rough edges are cut off, the board measures smaller. Your 1-inch board is really only ¾ inch thick.

1" X 6" BOARDS

|← 20" →|

|← 18½" →|

CUT TWO PIECES 20 INCHES LONG FOR THE SIDES AND ONE 18½ INCHES LONG FOR THE BOTTOM.

CUT TWO ENDS.

PUT YOUR TOOLBOX TOGETHER WITH WOOD SCREWS.

_____ Bear credit
_____ / _____ Date and signature for
_____ Arrow point credit

c. Use at least two tools listed in requirement *a* to fix something.

_____ Bear credit
_____ / _____ Date and signature for
_____ Arrow point credit

CUB SCOUT LEADER BALOO SAYS:
When you have completed all three requirements, have a parent or an adult sign here.

_____ / _____ Date and signature for achievement 20

Achievements

Build a Model

Model kits can be fun to put together. You can be proud of your model when it is finished. Most boys like to build models. Did you know that you might still be building models when you grow up?

Many grown-ups like to build models as a hobby. They build ships out of wood or large model train layouts they call *pikes*.

Models are also used by companies for serious purposes. Automakers build small models of their new cars before they actually start making them. Companies that build airplanes do the same things. People who design and build shopping centers and other buildings often build models to see what the building will look like. Model building can be serious business for grown-ups. As you can see, model building can be more than just going to the hobby shop and buying a kit.

REQUIREMENTS

Do three of the following requirements:

a. Build a model from a kit.

This can be any kind of model. Follow the directions, and feel free to change it any way you want to make it your own.

_____ Bear credit
_____ /_____ Date and signature for
_____ Arrow point credit

b. Build a display for one of your models.

If your model is a boat, mold soft clay into "waves" around the boat up to the water line. Remove the boat. After the clay has hardened, paint it blue and white to make it look like water with waves and whitecaps.

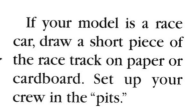

If your model is a race car, draw a short piece of the race track on paper or cardboard. Set up your crew in the "pits."

Achievements

If your model is a dinosaur, give it a natural setting by using clay, leaves, and twigs.

_____ Bear credit
_____ / _____ Date and signature for
_____ Arrow point credit

---

c. Pretend that you are planning to change the furniture layout in one of the rooms in your home.

Draw the outline of the room on a piece of paper. On another piece of paper draw the outlines of the furniture and cut them out. Draw your room and furniture cutouts to the scale of ½ inch = 1 foot. Use the paper cutouts on your room drawing to plan the changes. See how much easier it is to move your cutouts around than it is to move the furniture. Models let us see what the real thing will look like before it is made.

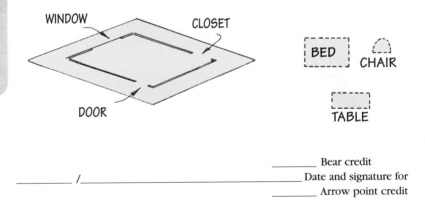

_____ Bear credit
_____ / _____ Date and signature for
_____ Arrow point credit

> **d. Make a model of a mountain, a meadow, a canyon, or a river.**

Use dirt, sand, stones, sticks, twigs, and grass cuttings.

_____ Bear credit
_____ / _____ Date and signature for
_____ Arrow point credit

> **e. Go and see a model of a shopping center or new building that is on display somewhere.**

That model might have been built to help plan the construction. It might also have been used to show the project to community leaders.

_____ Bear credit
_____ / _____ Date and signature for
_____ Arrow point credit

> **f. Make a model of a rocket, boat, car, or plane.**

Use whatever you want to make it.

_____ Bear credit
_____ / _____ Date and signature for
_____ Arrow point credit

CUB SCOUT LEADER BALOO SAYS:
When you have done three of the requirements, have a parent or an adult sign here.

_____/_____ Date and signature for
achievement 21

g It All Up

Sailors, cowboys, and mountain climbers all use good strong rope. Their lives sometimes depend on their ropes and the knots that hold them in place.

REQUIREMENTS

Do five of the following requirements:

> ### a. Whip the ends of a rope.

Ropes are made of twisted fibers. As long as the rope is in one piece, the fibers stay in place, but when the rope is cut, the fibers in the two ends begin to straighten out. Whip them in place with string or wrap them with tape.

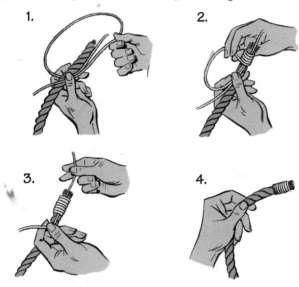

1.

2.

3.

4.

WHIP A ROPE.
Start with a 2-foot length of twine or cotton fishing line. Form it into a loop and place it at one end of the rope. Wrap the twine tightly around the rope, starting ¼ inch from the rope end. When the whipping is as wide as the rope is thick, pull out the ends hard and trim off the twine or fishing line.

_____ Bear credit
_____ / _____ Date and signature for
_____ Arrow point credit

> **b. Tie a square knot, bowline, sheet bend, two half hitches, and slip knot. Tell how each knot is used.**

SQUARE KNOT. A common knot made with two overhand knots. Square knots are used in first aid to tie bandages and to join two pieces of rope of the same thickness.

BOWLINE. A knot to make a nonslip loop at the end of a rope. It is a rescue knot when tied around the waist.

SHEET BEND. This knot looks like a bowline, but instead of making a loop, it joins ropes of different sizes.

TWO HALF HITCHES. This knot is used to tie a rope to a post, a tree, or a ring.

Achievements

SLIP KNOT. This knot slips easily along the rope around which it is made. The knot itself is a simple overhand knot. It can be used to tie a rope to a post.

_____ Bear credit

_____ / _____ Date and signature for

_____ Arrow point credit

---

c. Learn how to keep a rope from tangling.

Before you put a rope away, lay the rope out straight on a dry surface. Be sure there are no kinks or knots in it. Hold the end of the rope in one hand and coil the rope around your forearm from hand to elbow. Loop it around as many times as necessary to take up all of the rope. Take it off your elbow, hold the coil in your hand and take off the last loop with your other hand. Make a few turns around the coils with this end and pass it through the top of the coil held by your hand.

_____ Bear credit

_____ / _____ Date and signature for

_____ Arrow point credit

Put a weight on the end of your rope, heavy enough to carry your line out when you throw it.

Coil your rope in 1-foot loops. Hold half the loops and the weighted line in your throwing hand. Hold the other loops in your other hand.

Face the marker and swing the line toward it. Keep trying until you can hit the mark. It is important that you become good at this in case someday you need to rescue a person from drowning.

_____ Bear credit
_____ / _____ Date and signature for
_____ Arrow point credit

Achievements

e. Learn a magic rope trick.

Fold your arms across your chest, lean forward, and pick up one end of a rope in each hand. Unfold your arms and you have tied an over-hand knot.

MAN OVERBOARD. Hold one end of a rope in your left hand with your thumb up. With your right hand thumb down, grasp the rope and turn your hand thumb up to match your left hand. Transfer the loop from your right hand to your left. Continue to make loops in this way until you get near the end of the rope. Then pass the end of the rope through all of the loops. Ask someone to pull the end of the rope while you hold the loops loosely in both hands. As the rope runs out, overhand knots will appear in a chain of knots.

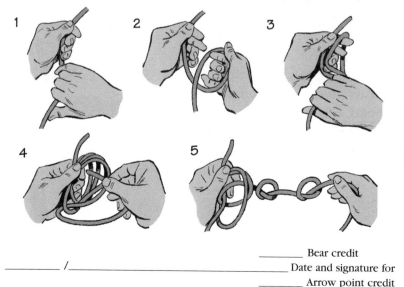

_____ Bear credit
_____ / _____ Date and signature for
_____ Arrow point credit

f. Make your own rope.

Use 24 feet of twine. Put the ends alongside each other and tie them in an overhand knot.

Soak the twine thoroughly before you start. Clamp a large nail in a bench vise and loop the knotted end of the twine over the nail.

Pull the twine loop out straight until you get to the end of the loop. Take the end of the loop back to the nail and place it over the nail and on top of the knotted end of the twine. Now pull back on the two loops to their ends.

Put the two loops on a hook that you have placed in a carpenter's drill brace. Using the brace and pulling back slightly to keep the twine tight, twist the four strands of twine together tightly until they choke up around the nail and the hook. Keep the twisting twine straight by pulling back on the brace.

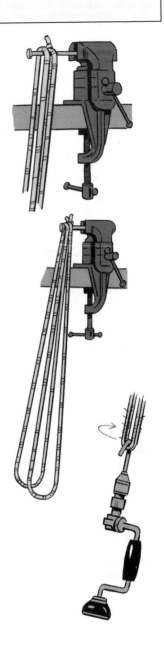

Place a chair or stool where you are standing and rest the brace on the seat. The weight of the brace will keep your new rope straight.

Now for the hard part: Let the rope dry for 24 hours. Then remove the nail and hook and whip each end.

With an adult's help, singe the loose fibers from the rope.

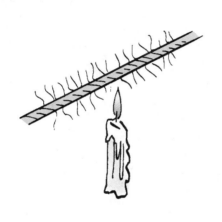

CUB SCOUT LEADER BALOO SAYS:
When you have done five of the requirements, have a parent or an adult sign here.

Sports, Sports, Sports!

Sports make for great times. They help us stay healthy and in good shape. They are fun to watch and fun to play.

REQUIREMENTS

Do all of the following requirements:

> ### a. Learn the rules of and how to play three team sports.

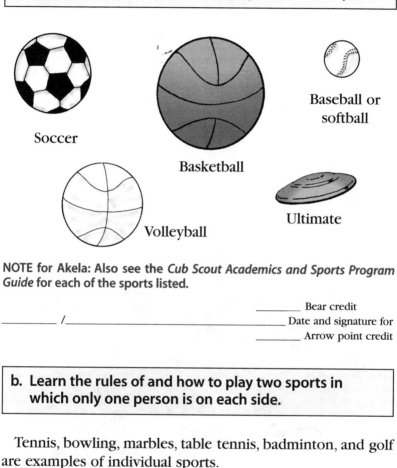

Soccer

Basketball

Baseball or softball

Volleyball

Ultimate

NOTE for Akela: Also see the *Cub Scout Academics and Sports Program Guide* for each of the sports listed.

_____ /_____

_____ Bear credit
_____ Date and signature for
_____ Arrow point credit

> ### b. Learn the rules of and how to play two sports in which only one person is on each side.

Tennis, bowling, marbles, table tennis, badminton, and golf are examples of individual sports.

NOTE for Akela: Also see the *Cub Scout Academics and Sports Program Guide* for each of the sports listed.

_____ /_____

_____ Bear credit
_____ Date and signature for
_____ Arrow point credit

c. Take part in one team and one individual sport.

_____ _____

Team Sport

_____ _____

Individual Sport

_____ Bear credit
_____ /_____ Date and signature for
_____ Arrow point credit

d. Watch a sport on TV with a parent or some other member of your family.

Discuss the rules and how the game was played.

_____ Bear credit
_____ /_____ Date and signature for
_____ Arrow point credit

The Bear Trail • Self

e. Attend a high school, college, or professional sporting event with your family or your den.

Did the players show good sportsmanship?

Did the spectators?

_____ / _____

_____ Bear credit
Date and signature for
_____ Arrow point credit

CUB SCOUT LEADER BALOO SAYS:
When you have done all the requirements, have a parent or an adult sign here.

_____ / _____ Date and signature for achievement 23

Achievements

Be a Leader

Leadership means more than just telling others what to do. It means doing the right things. It also means listening to everyone's ideas before going ahead.

It's hard to be a good leader, but you feel good if you do your job well.

Your community and country need good leaders. In these requirements you will find some ways to be a good leader.

REQUIREMENTS

Do three of the following requirements:

> **a. Help a boy join Cub Scouting or help a new Cub Scout through the Bobcat trail.**

Do you know any boys your age who are not Cub Scouts? Being interested in others is the mark of a leader.

_____ Bear credit
_____ /_____ Date and signature for
_____ Arrow point credit

> **b. Serve as a denner or assistant denner.**

Denner_____ from_____ to _____

Assistant
denner_____ from_____ to _____

_____ Bear credit
_____ /_____ Date and signature for
_____ Arrow point credit

> **c. Plan and conduct a den activity with the approval of your den leader.**

Den activity _____

_____

_____ Bear credit
_____ /_____ Date and signature for
_____ Arrow point credit

_____ / _____ Den leader's signature

d. Tell two people they have done a good job.

For example:
- A Cub Scout leads a good ceremony.

- A classmate does well on an assignment.

- A parent helps your den with an outing.

_____ Bear credit
_____ /_____ Date and signature for
_____ Arrow point credit

The Bear Trail • Self

> **e. Leadership means choosing a way even when not everybody likes your choice.**

Talk about these hard choices with a parent or another adult. What would you do if it were up to you?

- It is time to go home, but you are having a good time with your friends and they don't have to be home until 30 minutes later. What do you do?

- Your friends are going to ride their bikes to the other side of town, and they ask you to go with them. You know you are not allowed to do that. What do you say to them?

- A new boy has moved into the neighborhood. How do you become his friend?

- While your class is taking a test, the teacher leaves the room. Some of the students start trading test answers. Do you?

- What if another student asks you for an answer?

- Is it hard to keep from cheating?

_____ /_____
_____ Bear credit
_____ Date and signature for
_____ Arrow point credit

Achievements

CUB SCOUT LEADER BALOO SAYS:
When you have done three of the requirements, have a parent or an adult sign here.

_____ /_____ Date and signature for achievement 24

Now Follow My
Arrow Point Trail

Now you are a Bear Cub Scout. Wait! You can still have lots of fun with your *Bear Book*. Baloo has electives for you too. Electives are not like achievements. You can pick any requirement you like from the electives and do it. When you have completed ten elective requirements, you have earned your first Arrow Point—a gold one. After earning a Gold Arrow Point, you may complete ten more requirements to earn a Silver Arrow Point. Under your Bear badge, you may wear as many Silver Arrow Points as you earn.

When working on the achievements to earn your Bear badge, you might have seen some requirements you wanted to try but didn't. Now you can review the Achievements section of your *Bear Book* and use any requirement you did not count toward your Bear badge. These achievement requirements now follow the same rules as the elective requirements. Each one is a separate project. You can mix requirements from electives and unused achievements in any way to get the ten you need for each Arrow Point.

You may earn Arrow Points from the *Bear Cub Scout Book* until you become a Webelos Scout.

Remember these important rules: You may work on these electives all through your Bear year, but you cannot receive

Arrow Points until you have earned your Bear badge. Any achievement requirement that you completed to earn your Bear badge cannot be used again to earn Arrow Points, but there are many more to choose from.

Space

What do you see when you look toward the sky? You might say, "In the daytime, I see the sun and clouds. At night, I see the moon and stars."

That's true, of course. You also are looking at our world's newest frontier.

Here's your chance to learn something about space.

REQUIREMENTS

___a. Identify two constellations and the North Star.

___b. Make a pinhole planetarium and show three constellations.

___c. Visit a planetarium.

___d. Build a model of a rocket or space satellite.

___e. Read and talk about at least one man-made satellite and one natural one.

___f. Find a picture of another planet in our solar system. Explain how it is different from Earth.

NO.	DATE	ADULT SIGNATURE	✓DEN CHART
1.			
1.			
1.			
1.			
1.			
1.			

Arrow Point Trail

CONSTELLATIONS AND THE NORTH STAR

Groups of stars have names. One star group looks like a W. Another one, the Big Dipper, looks like a bit water dipper or saucepan. Two stars in the bowl of the Big Dipper point to the North Star. Make a pinhole planetarium with a tin can and a small nail. Punch tiny holes in the bottom of the can to mark each star's position in a constellation. Look through the pop-top hole in the top of the can while holding the bottom of the can toward a strong light.

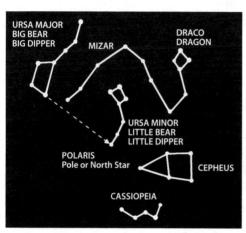

SATELLITES

Satellites are smaller objects that move around bigger ones. The moon is a satellite of Earth. Some of our TV and radio programs are brought to us by signals bounced off man-made satellites placed in orbit by the space shuttle.

Arrow Point Trail

Weather

Everybody wants to know what the weather is and what it will be tomorrow. Will it rain out my team's baseball game? Do I need a jacket? Those are questions you have probably asked.

In this elective, you will learn how weather forecasts are made, how to measure rainfall and snowfall, and how to figure wind directions.

REQUIREMENTS

____a. Learn how to read a thermometer. Put a thermometer outdoors and read it at the same time every day for 2 weeks. Keep a record of each day's temperature and a description of the weather each day (fair skies, rain, fog, snow, etc.).

____b. Build a weather vane. Record wind direction every day at the same hour for 2 weeks. Keep a record of the weather for each day.

____c. Make a rain gauge.

____d. Find out what a barometer is and how it works. Tell your den about it. Tell what relative humidity means.

____e. Learn to identify three different kinds of clouds. Estimate their heights.

____f. Watch the weather forecast on TV every day for 2 weeks. Describe three different symbols used on weather maps. Keep a record of how many times the weather forecast is correct.

This elective is also part of the World Conservation Award (see page 259).

NO.	DATE	ADULT SIGNATURE	✓ DEN CHART
2.			
2.			
2.			
2.			
2.			
2.			

NOTE for Akela: Also see the pages on weather in the *Cub Scout Academics and Sports Program Guide.*

OUTDOOR THERMOMETER

For your outdoor thermometer, build a box with pieces of an old slatted shutter for the sides. This will keep the sun away from it but let air in.

Set it up facing north. It should be about 4 feet off the ground so the thermometer will be easy for you to see. Read the temperature at the same time every day. Mark it on a chart like the one shown below.

DATE	TEMPERATURE	WEATHER	WIND

WEATHER VANE

Weather forecasters describe the wind by the direction it is coming from—not the direction in which it is going. The notched end of your vane points toward the direction the wind is coming from. If you forget, look at the smoke from chimneys and you can see it blowing away from the wind. Toss up a few blades of grass and see which way they go. Check the wind direction at the same time that you check your temperature and rain gauges. Mark it on your chart.

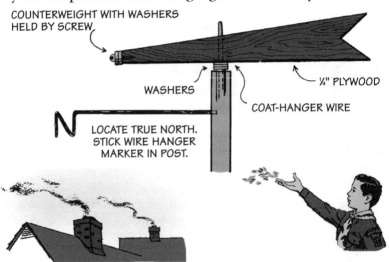

COUNTERWEIGHT WITH WASHERS HELD BY SCREW

WASHERS

¼" PLYWOOD

COAT-HANGER WIRE

LOCATE TRUE NORTH. STICK WIRE HANGER MARKER IN POST.

RAIN GAUGE

Use a large juice can (1 quart, 14 ounces). Set it on a platform with sides to keep it from blowing away. Choose an open place in your yard. Take your reading at the same time

CAN MUST BE LEVEL.

BE SURE CAN WON'T BLOW OFF.

CAN ABOUT 30" ABOVE GROUND.

TO MAKE MEASURING JAR, POUR 1" OF WATER IN THE JUICE CAN. THEN POUR IT IN A TALL OLIVE JAR AND MARK 1". DIVIDE INTO 10THS.

every day—morning, afternoon, or evening. If there is not enough water to measure in the can, pour it from the can into a measuring jar.

Snowfall can be measured by how much water it makes. Melt the snow collected and measure it in your measuring jar. One inch of water equals about 10 inches of snow.

You can measure snow on the ground by sticking a ruler or yardstick into several spots. Write each measurement down. Add them up and divide by the number of measurements. (Ask for help with this one.) This gives you the average depth of snow.

TYPES OF CLOUDS

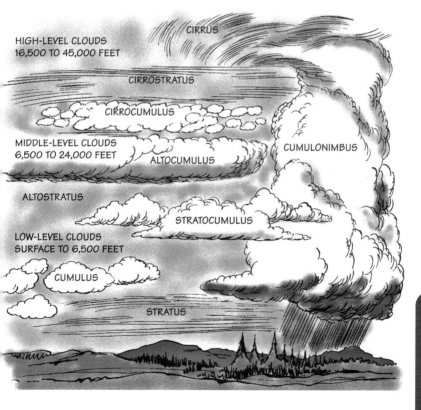

HIGH-LEVEL CLOUDS
16,500 TO 45,000 FEET

CIRRUS

CIRROSTRATUS

CIRROCUMULUS

MIDDLE-LEVEL CLOUDS
6,500 TO 24,000 FEET

ALTOCUMULUS

CUMULONIMBUS

ALTOSTRATUS

STRATOCUMULUS

LOW-LEVEL CLOUDS
SURFACE TO 6,500 FEET

CUMULUS

STRATUS

BAROMETER

Weather forecasters use a barometer to help predict whether it will rain or whether a nice day is coming. They can do this because the barometer measures air pressure.

Air pressure, or the weight of the air, helps them learn whether it will be fair or rainy. Warm air is lighter than cold air and is more likely to create a storm.

Early barometers were the mercury-in-a-tube kind. Modern barometers are smaller and easier to use. Air pressure can also be given in pounds per inch or in millibars. Average air pressure is less the higher you go, but at sea level it is 14.7 pounds per square inch.

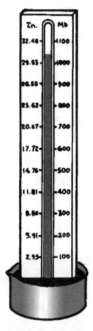

MERCURY BAROMETER

ANEROID BAROMETER

Arrow Point Trail

RELATIVE HUMIDITY

Relative humidity is the term weather forecasters use for the amount of moisture in the air. If there is a lot of moisture in the air, the relative humidity will be a high figure, like 70 or 80. If the air is dry, it will be much lower, like 20 or 30.

On a summer day, if the temperature is 85° and the relative humidity is 80, you will feel hot and sticky. On a day when it's cooler, that much humidity won't bother you at all. It will be a pleasant day.

The weather forecaster finds the figure for relative humidity by comparing the amount of moisture actually in the air with the most moisture the air could hold at the same temperature.

Radio

You probably hear a radio every day without thinking much about it. Radio is just one of the things you have grown up with.

When radio first began, however, everyone thought it was wonderful that music and words could be sent all over the world without wires.

You can find out for yourself the excitement of the early days of radio and learn how a radio works by building one for yourself.

REQUIREMENTS

> ____a. Build a crystal or diode radio. Check with your local craft or hobby shop or the nearest Scout shop that carries a crystal radio kit. It is all right to use a kit.
>
> ____b. Make and operate a battery-powered radio, following the directions with the kit.

NO.	DATE	ADULT SIGNATURE	✓ DEN CHART
3.			
3.			

Arrow Point Trail

The Arrow Point Trail

Many good kits are available for making crystal sets. This is the first kind of radio that was invented. They get their power from the radio signal, so you will need a long, high antenna to make yours work. Even with a good antenna, there will be enough power only for a small earphone.

A transistor radio also can be built from a kit. This kind of radio gets its power from a battery, so it might be able to operate a loudspeaker. Ask an adult to help you. Follow directions carefully, and you'll have a thrill of "tuning in on the world."

Hang a map on the wall (one you have pasted onto cardboard) and keep track of all the stations you get.

Maybe you know someone who is an amateur radio operator or "ham." Ask to see his or her transmitter and receiver. Ask about some of the faraway places he or she has contacted by radio.

TUNING COIL

GROUND

MINILABS

ANTENNA

EAR PHONE

Arrow Point Trail

Electricity

Wouldn't it be fun to make an electric motor that really works? Well, you can.

You can also make other things, like games and toys, that run on electricity.

As you build them, you will be learning about electricity—the power that runs so many things around your house and school and around your community.

REQUIREMENTS

____a. Wire a buzzer or doorbell.

____b. Make an electric buzzer game.

____c. Make a simple bar or horseshoe electromagnet.

____d. Use a simple electric motor.

____e. Make a crane with an electromagnetic lift.

NO.	DATE	ADULT SIGNATURE	✓ DEN CHART
4.			
4.			
4.			
4.			
4.			

Did your doorbell ever quit working? Sometimes when that happens, it's just because the connections are loose or the wires are corroded. If you know how to wire a doorbell, you will probably know how to fix it. You can mount a doorbell buzzer on a piece of wood to learn how to wire it. Get someone to work with you on this.

Electromagnets take some skill to make but are a lot of fun. You can make all kinds of tools and electric games with them. Get an adult to work with you on this.

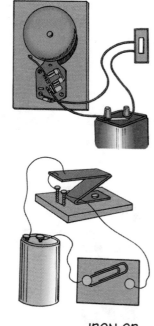

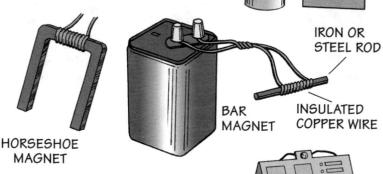

HORSESHOE
MAGNET

BAR
MAGNET

INSULATED
COPPER WIRE

IRON OR
STEEL ROD

Make up a separate sounding board. This can be used for many games. Make a question-and-answer board for your teacher. You can use it for many different quizzes. Write the questions and answers on sticky tape, and you can change them as often as you wish.

Any number of electric games can be made using a buzzer, a bell, or a flashlight bulb. A few basic types are shown. Now invent your own.

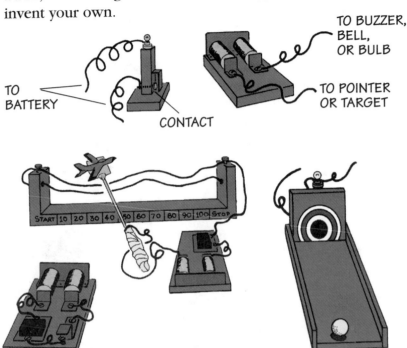

TO BUZZER,
BELL,
OR BULB

TO
BATTERY

TO POINTER
OR TARGET

CONTACT

How to Make a Tin-Can Motor

Using the rotor pattern on page 173, cut five pieces of tin. Drill a center hole to fit snugly on a 2¼-inch finishing nail. Fasten the five pieces together with adhesive tape.

Wind magnet wire on the rotor until the space is nearly full. Leave 2-inch lengths of wire at the ends of the winding.

Wind ½-inch adhesive tape on the nail close to the rotor to form the commutator. Wind the tape until it is about ¼ inch thick. Cut two ½-by-¼-inch tin strips to mold around the adhesive tape, each covering about one-fourth of the surface. Scrape the wire ends of the winding and wrap each end around one of the tin strips. Fasten in place with ⅛-inch strips of adhesive tape.

The Arrow Point Trail

Cut a 3¾-by-9-inch strip of tin, fold it five times to ¾ inch width, and hammer it flat. Bend it to the shape shown below to form the field bracket.

Wind several layers of wire around the top of the field, leaving a few inches of wire on each side for connections.

The brushes are made from strand wire wrapped around tin strips. Connect the field wire to the base. Fold tin strips to ½ inch width to form the uprights. Put a hole in each upright to support the nail. For power, connect to three dry batteries or a toy transformer.

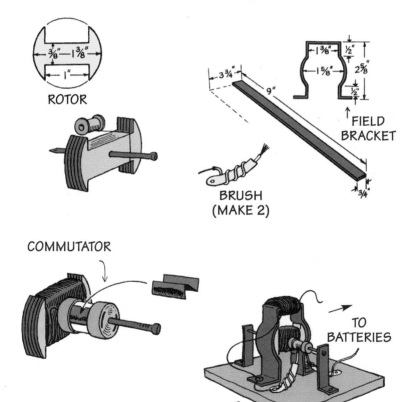

ROTOR

FIELD BRACKET

BRUSH (MAKE 2)

COMMUTATOR

TO BATTERIES

FIELD BRUSHES AND ASSEMBLY

Boats

Boating and sailing are great sports. Maybe you've already been sailing, but do you know how to rig a sailboat? Make a raft? Repair a dock? Do you know the safety rules for boating? If your answers were no, find out now. Anchors aweigh!

REQUIREMENTS

___a. Help an adult rig and sail a real boat.

___b. Help an adult repair a real boat or canoe.

___c. Know the flag signals for storm warnings.

___d. Help an adult repair a boat dock.

___e. Know the rules of boat safety.

___f. With an adult, demonstrate forward strokes, turns, and backstrokes. Row a boat around a 100-yard course involving two turns.

NO.	DATE	ADULT SIGNATURE	✓ DEN CHART
5.			
5.			
5.			
5.			
5.			
5.			

Arrow Point Trail

SAILBOATS

Sailing is a fine sport. Help an adult rig and sail a real boat— one you can ride in.

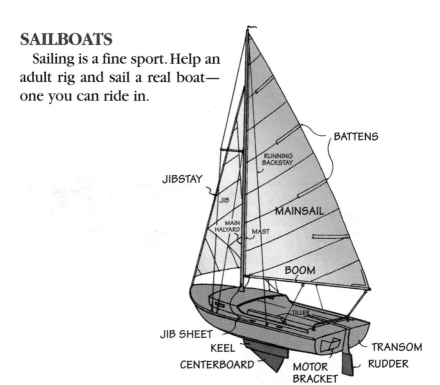

BATTENS

RUNNING BACKSTAY

JIBSTAY

JIB

MAINSAIL

MAIN HALYARD

MAST

BOOM

TILLER

JIB SHEET

KEEL

CENTERBOARD

MOTOR BRACKET

TRANSOM

RUDDER

REPAIRING A DOCK

You get credit in this elective by helping your parent or any other adult fix up a boat dock. Check for boards that are loose, nails that are sticking up, or splintery wood that could cause an accident and injure someone.

CANOES

Repairing a boat or canoe is a good thing to be able to do. You'll be a proud Cub Scout if you're able to help a boat owner make repairs. Follow his or her instructions.

WOOD CANOE

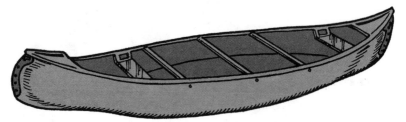

ALUMINUM CANOE

FIBERGLASS CANOE

STORM WARNINGS

The Weather Bureau uses a combination of flags and pennants to warn boaters of approaching storms.

Small-Craft Warning. One red flag by day and a red light above a white light at night.

SMALL
CRAFT

Gale Warning. Two red pennants by day and a white light above a red light at night.

GALE

Whole-Gale Warning. A single square red flag with a black center by day and two red lights at night.

WHOLE
GALE

Hurricane Warning. Two square red flags with black centers by day and a white light between two red lights at night.

HURRICANE

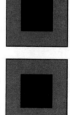

Arrow Point Trail

ROWING

Grasp the oar handles firmly, knuckles up, wrists and arms straight, body bent forward.

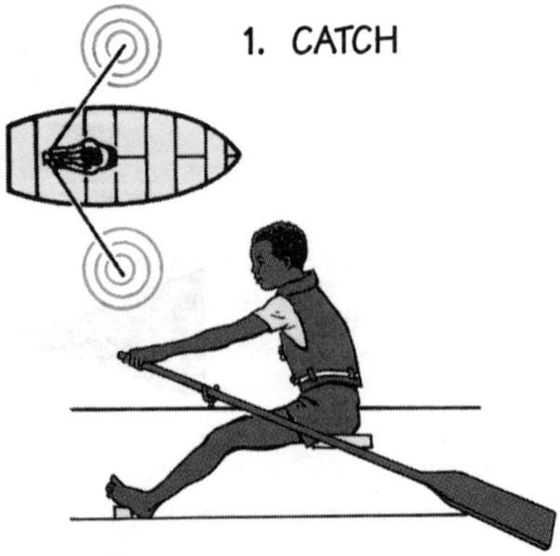

Catch. Lower the oar blades edgewise into the water, not too deep.

Pull. Lean backward, pulling on the oars and bending your arms until your elbows come in against your ribs.

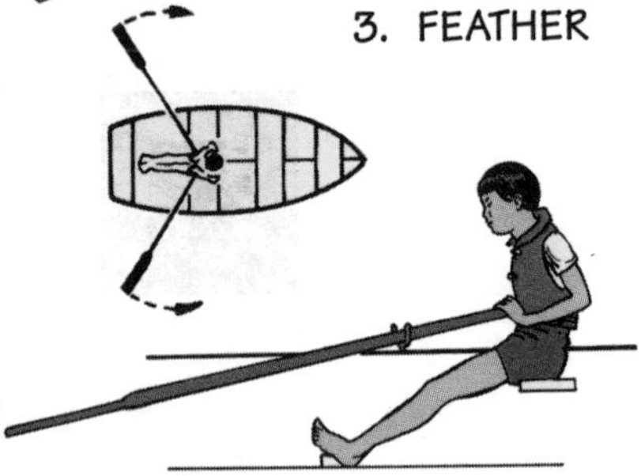

Feather. Lift the oar blades slightly out of the water and turn your knuckles up toward your face so that the blades are flat on the water's surface.

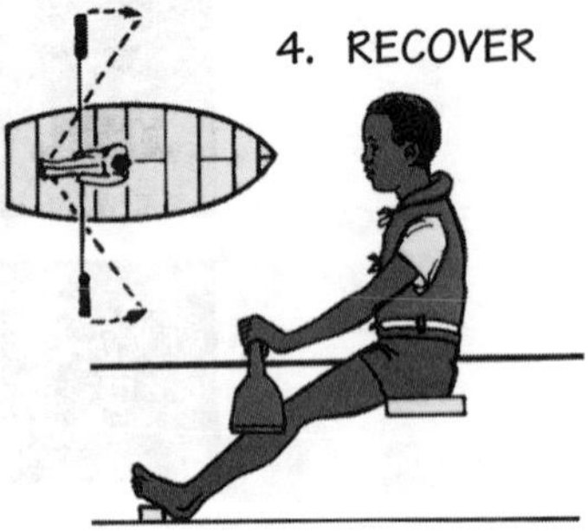

Recover. Bend forward and straighten your wrists and arms, ready to begin another stroke.

To do the backstroke, push on the oars instead of pulling.

1. CATCH

2. PULL

3. FEATHER

4. RECOVER

To turn, pull on one oar while you hold the other in the water as a pivot or push it in the opposite direction.

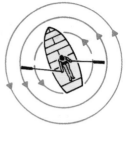

TURNING

Boat Safety Rules

1. Know your boat—don't overload it. In a rowboat, one person per seat is a fairly safe rule.

2. Balance your load. Distribute weight evenly from side to side and from bow to stern.

3. Step into your boat. Step in the center when boarding or changing seats, keeping low. Each passenger in the boat should wear a personal flotation device.

4. If your boat capsizes or swamps, hang on. You can kick the boat to shore or drift in, but don't leave it. Let help come to you.

5. Watch the weather. Head for shore when it looks stormy. If you are caught out, seat your passengers on the floor and head your boat into the waves.

6. If you use a motor, use the right one. Too much power can damage your boat or swamp it. Look on your boat's transom for the OBC (Outboard Boating Club of America) plate showing boat capacity and recommended maximum horsepower. Avoid sharp turns—they are hard on equipment and people. Take it easy.

Aircraft

Cub Scouts can learn a lot about airplanes and flying.

They can fly model airplanes. They can visit airports, talk to pilots, and be passengers in airplanes.

There are lots of ways to have fun with airplanes and to learn more about them.

REQUIREMENTS

____a. Identify five different kinds of aircraft, in flight if possible, or from models or photos.

____b. Ride in an airplane (commercial or private).

____c. Explain how a hot-air balloon works.

____d. Build and fly a model airplane. (You may use a kit. Every time you do this differently, it counts as a completed project.)

____e. Sketch and label an airplane showing the direction of forces acting on it (lift, drag, and load.)

____f. Make a list of some of the things a helicopter can do that other kinds of aircraft can't. Draw or cut out a picture of a helicopter and label the parts.

____g. Build and display a scale model airplane. You may use a kit or build it from plans.

NO.	DATE	ADULT SIGNATURE	✓ DEN CHART
6.			
6.			
6.			
6.			
6.			
6.			
6.			

HOT-AIR BALLOONS

The first successful flying machines were hot-air balloons. We fly them today for sport, but they still work the same way.

Air has weight, just like everything else made of matter. Air, and other gases, expand when they are heated. A plastic bag of hot air will weigh less than a plastic bag of cool air. The plastic bag of hot air will try to rise like a bubble in water because the cooler, heavier air around it tries to push in and occupy the same space. This is how a hot-air balloon works. Some balloons use other kinds of gas, such as helium, which is already lighter than air without being heated.

Arrow Point Trail

THERMALS

When the sun heats the ground, a layer of air near the surface is heated too and rises in a current of warm air called a thermal. In the same way, warm air from a fire rises up the chimney, drawing in fresh air for the fire and carrying the smoke away. Sailplane pilots find these invisible rising currents and ride them.

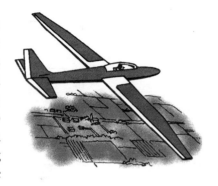

TYPES OF AIRCRAFT

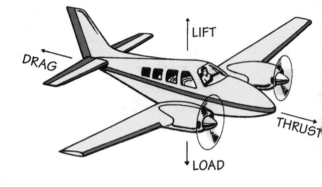

The space shuttle flies like an airplane when it lands.

Arrow Point Trail

MODEL AIRPLANES

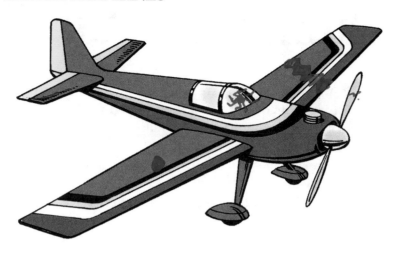

Many stores sell kits for making scale model airplanes that fly and solid models that don't. The kits have instructions for putting the parts together. After a little practice with these, you can design and build your own special model.

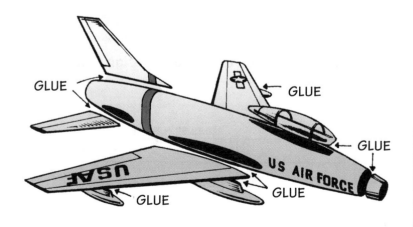

GLUE

GLUE

GLUE

GLUE

GLUE

US AIR FORCE

USAF

Things That Go 7

Maybe when you were little, your folks got you a toy car to ride. It was lots of fun. Think how much fun it would be now to build your own! You can build it any way you like, and stop, go, or steer as you please.

On the next page you'll see plans for your Cubmobile. Try it and have fun.

Cubmobiles are not the only things that go. Have you ever seen a windmill or a waterwheel and wondered what they do? Here are plans for windmills and waterwheels that you can make. After you've made them, you might want to invent something of your own that goes.

REQUIREMENTS

___a. Make a scooter or a Cubmobile. Know the safety rules.

___b. Make a windmill.

___c. Make a waterwheel.

___d. Make an invention of your own design that goes.

NO.	DATE	ADULT SIGNATURE	✓ DEN CHART
7.			
7.			
7.			
7.			

Arrow Point Trail

The Arrow Point Trail

CUBMOBILE. Use a helmet and safety belt.

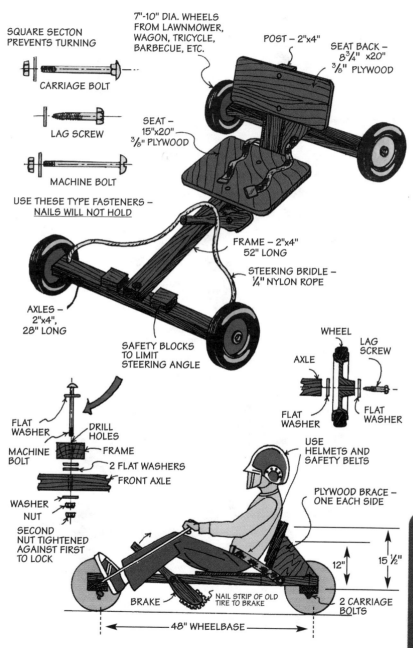

SQUARE SECTON PREVENTS TURNING

CARRIAGE BOLT

LAG SCREW

MACHINE BOLT

USE THESE TYPE FASTENERS – NAILS WILL NOT HOLD

7"-10" DIA. WHEELS FROM LAWNMOWER, WAGON, TRICYCLE, BARBECUE, ETC.

POST – 2"x4"

SEAT BACK – 8¾" x20" ⅜" PLYWOOD

SEAT – 15"x20" ⅜" PLYWOOD

FRAME – 2"x4" 52" LONG

STEERING BRIDLE – ¼" NYLON ROPE

AXLES – 2"x4", 28" LONG

SAFETY BLOCKS TO LIMIT STEERING ANGLE

WHEEL

LAG SCREW

AXLE

FLAT WASHER

FLAT WASHER

FLAT WASHER

DRILL HOLES

MACHINE BOLT

FRAME

2 FLAT WASHERS

FRONT AXLE

WASHER

NUT

SECOND NUT TIGHTENED AGAINST FIRST TO LOCK

USE HELMETS AND SAFETY BELTS

PLYWOOD BRACE – ONE EACH SIDE

12"

15½"

BRAKE

NAIL STRIP OF OLD TIRE TO BRAKE

2 CARRIAGE BOLTS

48" WHEELBASE

Elective 7

185

Arrow Point Trail

SCOOTER

Sidewalk Safety Rules

- Pedestrians have the right-of-way.
- Watch out for cars coming out of driveways.
- Don't carry passengers.
- Don't ride in the street.

WINDMILL

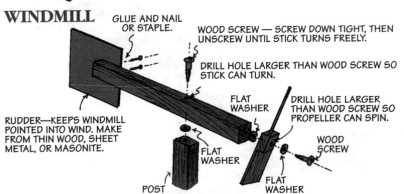

GLUE AND NAIL OR STAPLE.

WOOD SCREW — SCREW DOWN TIGHT, THEN UNSCREW UNTIL STICK TURNS FREELY.

DRILL HOLE LARGER THAN WOOD SCREW SO STICK CAN TURN.

FLAT WASHER

DRILL HOLE LARGER THAN WOOD SCREW SO PROPELLER CAN SPIN.

WOOD SCREW

RUDDER—KEEPS WINDMILL POINTED INTO WIND. MAKE FROM THIN WOOD, SHEET METAL, OR MASONITE.

FLAT WASHER

POST

FLAT WASHER

FLAT WASHER

PEOPLE HAVE USED WINDMILLS FOR THOUSANDS OF YEARS TO GRIND GRAIN AND PUMP WATER. TODAY WE ARE LEARNING TO USE THE WIND TO MAKE ELECTRIC POWER. WINDMILL BLADES MUST BE AT AN ANGLE TO THE DIRECTION OF THE WIND TO WORK. THE FASTER THE WIND BLOWS, THE FASTER YOUR WINDMILL WILL TURN.

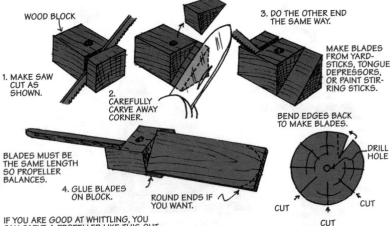

WOOD BLOCK

3. DO THE OTHER END THE SAME WAY.

MAKE BLADES FROM YARD-STICKS, TONGUE DEPRESSORS, OR PAINT STIR-RING STICKS.

1. MAKE SAW CUT AS SHOWN.

2. CAREFULLY CARVE AWAY CORNER.

BLADES MUST BE THE SAME LENGTH SO PROPELLER BALANCES.

BEND EDGES BACK TO MAKE BLADES.

DRILL HOLE

4. GLUE BLADES ON BLOCK.

ROUND ENDS IF YOU WANT.

CUT

CUT

IF YOU ARE GOOD AT WHITTLING, YOU CAN CARVE A PROPELLER LIKE THIS OUT OF A SOLID BLOCK OF SOFT WOOD.

CUT

YOU CAN ALSO MAKE A PROPELLER FROM A TIN CAN LID. MAKE 8 CUTS WITH TIN SNIPS (WEAR HEAVY COTTON WORK GLOVES) AND BEND EDGES BACK TO MAKE BLADES.

Arrow Point Trail

WATERWHEEL

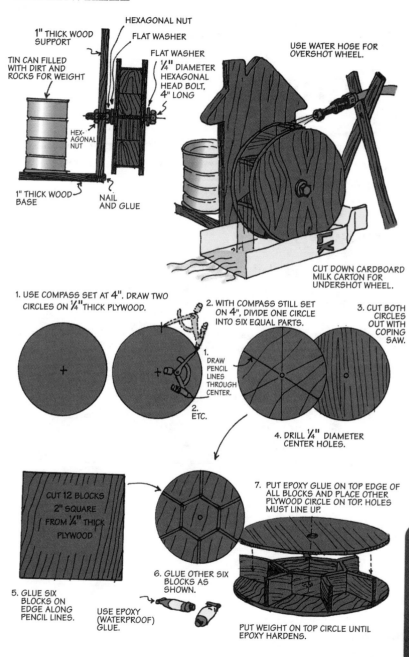

1" THICK WOOD SUPPORT

HEXAGONAL NUT

FLAT WASHER

FLAT WASHER
¼" DIAMETER
HEXAGONAL
HEAD BOLT,
4" LONG

TIN CAN FILLED
WITH DIRT AND
ROCKS FOR WEIGHT

USE WATER HOSE FOR
OVERSHOT WHEEL.

HEX-
AGONAL
NUT

1" THICK WOOD
BASE

NAIL
AND GLUE

CUT DOWN CARDBOARD
MILK CARTON FOR
UNDERSHOT WHEEL.

1. USE COMPASS SET AT 4". DRAW TWO
CIRCLES ON ¼" THICK PLYWOOD.

2. WITH COMPASS STILL SET
ON 4", DIVIDE ONE CIRCLE
INTO SIX EQUAL PARTS.

3. CUT BOTH
CIRCLES
OUT WITH
COPING
SAW.

1. DRAW
PENCIL
LINES
THROUGH
CENTER.

2.
ETC.

4. DRILL ¼" DIAMETER
CENTER HOLES.

CUT 12 BLOCKS
2" SQUARE
FROM ¼" THICK
PLYWOOD

7. PUT EPOXY GLUE ON TOP EDGE OF
ALL BLOCKS AND PLACE OTHER
PLYWOOD CIRCLE ON TOP. HOLES
MUST LINE UP.

6. GLUE OTHER SIX
BLOCKS AS
SHOWN.

5. GLUE SIX
BLOCKS ON
EDGE ALONG
PENCIL LINES.

USE EPOXY
(WATERPROOF)
GLUE.

PUT WEIGHT ON TOP CIRCLE UNTIL
EPOXY HARDENS.

Cub Scout Band

Here comes the band—the Cub Scout band!

You can play music even if you have never had a lesson. You can even make your own instrument. Learn how in this elective.

Strike up the band!

REQUIREMENTS

___a. Make and play a homemade musical instrument—cigar-box banjo, washtub bull fiddle, a drum or rhythm set, tambourine, etc.

___b. Learn to play two familiar tunes on an ocarina, a harmonica, or a tonette.

___c. Play in a den band using homemade or regular musical instruments. Play at a pack meeting.

___d. Play two tunes on any recognized band or orchestra instrument.

NO.	DATE	ADULT SIGNATURE	✓ DEN CHART
8.			
8.			
8.			
8.			

NOTE for Akela: Also see the pages on music in the *Cub Scout Academics and Sports Program Guide.*

All you need to get started is the desire to learn to play music. Try the simple instruments first until you find one you would like to play well. Then, practice!

If you are lucky enough to be studying with a music teacher, keep it up. Remember, you must practice to play well.

HOMEMADE MUSICAL INSTRUMENTS

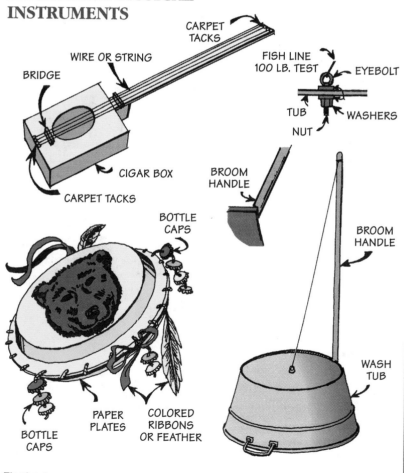

CARPET TACKS

WIRE OR STRING

BRIDGE

FISH LINE 100 LB. TEST

EYEBOLT

TUB

WASHERS

NUT

CIGAR BOX

CARPET TACKS

BROOM HANDLE

BROOM HANDLE

BOTTLE CAPS

WASH TUB

BOTTLE CAPS

PAPER PLATES

COLORED RIBBONS OR FEATHER

Arrow Point Trail

STICKS, BONES, and BLOCKS.
Use ½-inch and 1-inch dowels, 8 and 12 inches long. Notch some of them. Clean and dry short ribs of beef. Make hand-size sandpaper blocks.

RATTLES. Use gourds, spice boxes, small cans, shells, coconuts, paper tubes, or paper sacks for rattles. Put dried beans, peas, noodles, macaroni, sand, buttons, or beads in them.

TRIANGLES. Use a 12-inch-long brass pipe. Strike it with a 6-inch-long solid brass rod. Also use a horseshoe and spike and a pencil in a glass.

DRUMS. Use canvas, inner tube, or animal skin for drum heads. The drum body could be a tin can, ice-cream carton, cereal box, fiber drainpipe, or plastic pipe.

BOTTLE FLUTE. Place empty bottles on a tray in order of size. When you blow into the bottles, each one sounds different. Tune by adding water and adjusting the water levels.

Bottles are tuned, rubber bands are all in place, strings are tightened up, the washboard is handy—okay, strike up the band! Homemade bands are lots of fun. With a little practice you can get great music out of the simplest things.

Go to your library for more ideas or ask your music teacher for suggestions of instruments to make.

Art

Art is not just pictures. An artist's skill is used to make pictures and sculptures that tell a story and are pleasant to look at. That is what art is all about. Statues and stained glass windows are made for the same reasons. Study the art around you, and try your hand at making your own.

REQUIREMENTS

___a. **Do an original art project and show it at a pack meeting. Every project you do counts as one requirement. Here are some ideas for art projects:**

Mobile or wire sculpture   Collage
Silhouette   Mosaic
Acrylic painting   Clay sculpture
Watercolor painting   Silk screen picture

___b. **Visit an art museum or picture gallery with your den or family.**

NO.	DATE	ADULT SIGNATURE	✓ DEN CHART
9.			
9.			
9.			
9.			
9.			
9.			

Arrow Point Trail

MOBILE

To make a mobile you will need:

- Three pieces of coat-hanger wire, different lengths
- Four cardboard shapes (any shape you like)
- Heavy thread or light fishing line
- Fisherman's swivel
- Pair of pliers
- Ice pick or nail for punching holes in cardboard

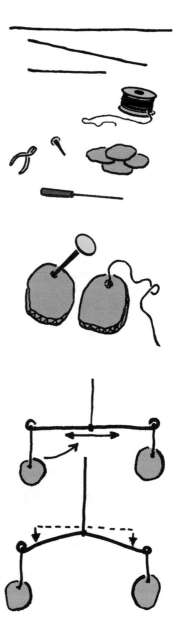

Step 1. Use the pliers to form a small loop in both ends of each piece of wire.

Step 2. Make one hole near the edge of each cardboard shape with the nail or ice pick. Tie a short piece of line to each cardboard piece.

Step 3. Tie one cardboard shape to each loop on the shortest piece of wire. Tie an 8-inch piece of line at the center.

Step 4. Slide the wire back and forth until it balances on the center line. Bend it at the balance point. This forms an angle that keeps the line from sliding back and forth.

Step 5. Tie this assembly to one end of the medium-length wire. Tie a cardboard shape to the other end. Tie an 8-inch line in the middle. Balance and bend the same way you did in step 4.

Step 6. Repeat step 5, using the longest wire and the assembly you made in step 5. Tie the hanging line to the fisherman's swivel. Use it to hang your mobile where it will be free to turn in air currents. The slightest breeze will make it turn and form ever-changing patterns.

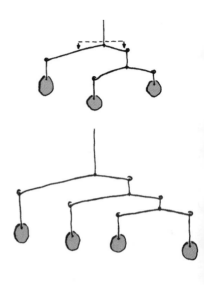

COLLAGE

A collage is a picture made up of bits of other pictures. The pieces are pasted down to make a new piece of art.

Arrow Point Trail

SILHOUETTE

Tape a piece of white paper to an easel or a door. Seat your subject between the paper and a bright light; his or her shadow will be cast onto the paper. Trace around the shadow with a pencil. Take the piece of paper down, lay it on a

sheet of black construction paper, and cut through both sheets along the pencil line you have traced. Paste the black silhouette cutout on a piece of white paper for display.

MOSAIC

A mosaic is a picture made of tiny bits of stone, tile, or glass cemented into a pattern. You can also glue seeds to a piece of plywood to make your mosaic. Use white glue or craft glue.

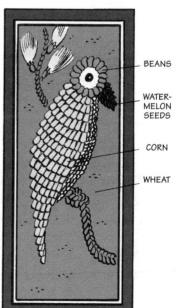

BEANS

WATER-
MELON
SEEDS

CORN

WHEAT

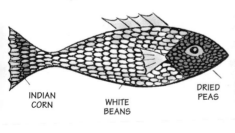

INDIAN
CORN

WHITE
BEANS

DRIED
PEAS

Masks

Since time began, we have been using masks in plays, games, and important religious ceremonies. We wear masks to pretend we are something besides ourselves. This can be fun, like on Halloween.

REQUIREMENTS

___a. Make a simple papier-mâché mask.

___b. Make an animal mask.

___c. Make a clown mask.

NO.	DATE	ADULT SIGNATURE	✓ DEN CHART
10.			
10.			
10.			

PAPIER-MÂCHÉ MASKS

The mask shown can be made on an oval dish. Turn the dish upside down and grease it so the mask won't stick when you're through. Tear newspapers into strips. Make a paste with flour and water. Make it quite thick—about as thick as

split pea soup. Now you are ready. Dip the paper strips into the paste mixture and lay them over the dish, overlapping and in different directions. Allow each layer to dry before adding another.

To build up the eyebrows, nose, lips, and cheeks, hold wads of newspaper in place and paste them down with long strips of paper.

After the mask is dry, paint the features. You can use a rubber ball for the clown's nose and rope, yarn, or brown straw for hair.

PAPER-BAG MASKS

Use a large grocery bag. Cut eyeholes and draw the face with a felt-tip pen. Cut another bag into strips. Curl the strips and glue them to the lion's head to make the lion's mane.

Glue two bags together to make a bull's head.

STYROFOAM OR CARDBOARD →

GLUE TWO SACKS TOGETHER TO MAKE NOSE.

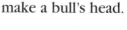

MILK JUG MASKS

Cut the milk jug in two with a knife or scissors. Trim off the top where the cap screws on. Each half can be used top- or bottom-side up to give you different face shapes.

The handle side (handle up) can be used for a knight's helmet, or for an "iron mask," sprayed with metallic paint. Remove a portion or all of the handle, add cardboard ears, and you have a dog, bear, or other animal. Turn it over and paint it gold—it looks like an Egyptian pharaoh with a high forehead and ornamental head covering. Paint it orange; add black stripes, pointed ears, a cardboard nose, and presto! A tiger. Painted black with broom-straw whiskers, a "purr-fectly" terrific cat appears.

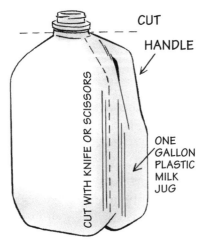

CUT

HANDLE

CUT WITH KNIFE OR SCISSORS

ONE GALLON PLASTIC MILK JUG

TIGER

PHARAOH

Arrow Point Trail

The other half can be used to make an owl, bird, or space creature. Make a knight or a clown, or paint it green to make a Martian. Many other characters can be made from this half.

Cut out eyeholes and mouth shapes with a knife or model-building knife. Glue on construction paper or felt decorations. Use your imagination; glue on bits of Styrofoam, yarn, fake fur, toothpaste caps, toothpicks, soda straws, or whatever you can find.

FOZZIE BEAR

Photography

Taking pictures is a lot of fun, but it can be harder than you might think. You need to use a camera to learn the secrets of taking good pictures.

REQUIREMENTS

____a. Practice holding a camera still in one position. Learn to push the shutter button without moving the camera. Do this without film in the camera until you have learned how. Look through the viewfinder and see what your picture will look like. Make sure that everything you want in your picture is in the frame of your viewfinder.

____b. Take five pictures of the same subject in different kinds of light.
   1. Subject in direct sun with direct light
   2. Subject in direct sun with side light
   3. Subject in direct sun with back light
   4. Subject in shade on a sunny day
   5. Subject on a cloudy day

____c. Put your pictures to use.
   1. Mount a picture on cardboard for display.
   2. Mount a picture on cardboard and give it to a friend.
   3. Make three pictures that show how something happened (tell a story) and write a one-sentence explanation for each.

____d. Take a picture in your house.
   1. With available light
   2. Using a flash attachment or photoflood (bright light)

NO.	DATE	ADULT SIGNATURE	✓ DEN CHART
11.			
11.			
11.			
11.			

IMPROVE YOUR PHOTOS BY CROPPING.

Crop (or trim) your pictures so they show only the main subjects. Crop out background that does not matter.

BEFORE CROPPING

AFTER CROPPING

The more pictures you take, the more you will notice that the ones you like best are the ones that tell a story. The subject is doing something besides posing. The action tells something about the subject.

Picture Hints

- Take the picture in bright light, if possible.
- Keep the camera steady.
- Wind the film right after you snap the picture.
- Remember that every good picture has a center of interest.
- Try to take the picture of your subject against a good background.
- Store negatives in transparent envelopes, not regular paper ones.

BACK LIGHT   SIDE LIGHT   DIRECT SUN

TOO FAR AWAY

DON'T TILT
THE CAMERA

GOOD

BUSY BACKGROUND

CONTRAST GOOD

AGAINST A POST

ON A ROCK OR CHAIR

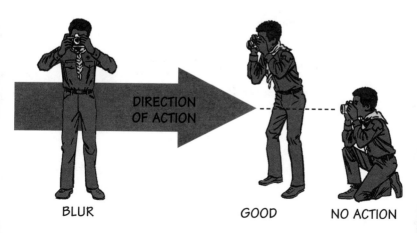

DIRECTION OF ACTION

BLUR

GOOD

NO ACTION

Arrow Point Trail

Nature Crafts

Nature is a fun world to get to know.

When you go on a hike with a group in the woods, watch for animal tracks. Look at the trees and see how many you can name. If you look carefully, you will see that the rocks are many shapes, sizes, and colors.

REQUIREMENTS

____a. Make shadow prints or blueprints of three kinds of leaves.

____b. Make a display of eight different animal tracks with an eraser print.

____c. Collect, press, and label ten kinds of leaves.

____d. Build a waterscope and identify five types of water life.

____e. Collect eight kinds of plant seeds and label them.

____f. Collect, mount, and label ten kinds of rocks or minerals.

____g. Collect, mount, and label five kinds of shells.

____h. Build and use a bird caller.

This elective is also part of the World Conservation Award (see page 259).

NO.	DATE	ADULT SIGNATURE	✓ DEN CHART
12.			
12.			
12.			
12.			
12.			
12.			
12.			
12.			

BLUEPRINTS

You can buy blueline or blueprint paper at a blueprint or surveyor supply store. Light will ruin the paper, so keep it covered until you are ready to use it. Place a leaf on glass and cover it with the blueprint paper (yellow side down). Place cardboard on top of the paper and use clothespins to hold it all together. Turn the stack over and expose it to sunlight for about 10 seconds. Turn it over again and carefully roll the paper and put it in a cardboard tube so it is not exposed to more light. Place the tube over a jar lid filled with ammonia to develop your leaf print.

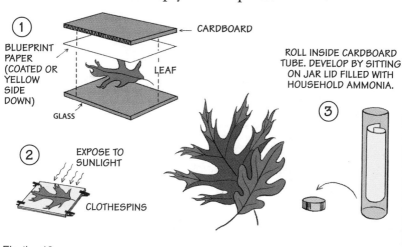

(1) CARDBOARD
BLUEPRINT PAPER (COATED OR YELLOW SIDE DOWN)
LEAF
GLASS

ROLL INSIDE CARDBOARD TUBE. DEVELOP BY SITTING ON JAR LID FILLED WITH HOUSEHOLD AMMONIA.

(3)

(2) EXPOSE TO SUNLIGHT
CLOTHESPINS

Arrow Point Trail

Elective 12

ERASER PRINTS

Use a stamp pad and a pencil eraser to print animal tracks. Study the animal tracks you find in the sand and mud along streams and mud puddles.

SHELL AND ROCK COLLECTIONS

Keep your collection in empty egg cartons. This will protect the shells from breakage. It will keep rocks from scratching shelves or furniture. Label each item.

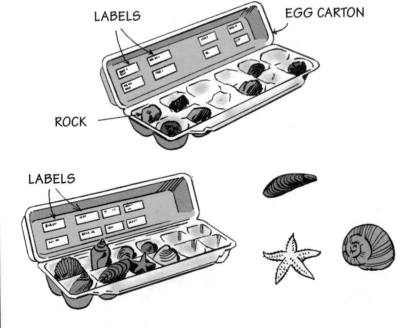

LABELS   EGG CARTON

ROCK

LABELS

WATERSCOPE

A waterscope will allow you to see water life more clearly. All you need are some tin cans, a plastic or glass jar, some wire, and some waterproof tape. Note five different examples of water life you see when using your new waterscope in a small stream or pond. Make sure an adult is with you.

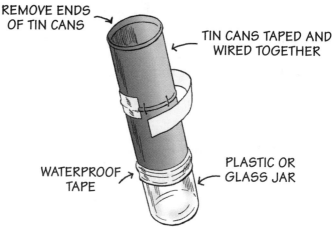

REMOVE ENDS OF TIN CANS

TIN CANS TAPED AND WIRED TOGETHER

WATERPROOF TAPE

PLASTIC OR GLASS JAR

BIRD CALLER

A bird caller requires a piece of hardwood about 2 inches long and 1 inch square. Obtain a screw eye. In one end of the wood, drill a hole slightly smaller than the threads of the screw. Turn the screw eye into the wood, take it out, and put some powdered resin in the hole. When the screw eye is turned back and forth, it will make a squeaky sound that attracts birds.

Arrow Point Trail

Magic

Now you see it—now you don't. Magic is a world of surprises. You can have fun with magic tricks.

REQUIREMENTS

___a. Learn and show three magic tricks.

___b. With your den, put on a magic show for someone else.

___c. Learn and show four puzzles.

___d. Learn and show three rope tricks.

NO.	DATE	ADULT SIGNATURE	✓ DEN CHART
13.			
13.			
13.			
13.			

Look in your *Boys' Life* magazines and *Cub Scout Magic* for more magic tricks.

STRING THE WASHERS

Knot one washer onto the center of a string as shown. Next, raise the two ends of the string and drop the rest of the washers on so that they fall onto the knotted washer.

Separate the two ends of the string and hand them to a helper.

Place a handkerchief over the washers. Reach under the handkerchief and pull the loop down over the last washer to release the knot. Pull all the washers out.

The trick is in tying the knot.

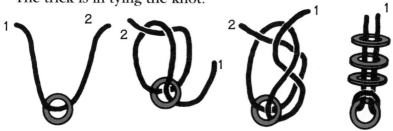

TRIANGLE TURNABOUT PUZZLE

Put ten checkers or ten coins on a table. Arrange them in a triangle pointing toward you. Don't put them close together (figure 1).

Tell the audience that the checkers or coins are flying saucers leaving their home bases. Say that they want to turn around and fly back home. Only three of them can fly in straight lines to make a new triangle pointing away from you.

Let the audience have plenty of time to try to do it. Remember, they can move only three items, and all must move in straight lines.

Show them how by making the moves shown in figures 2, 3, and 4.

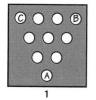

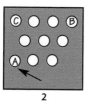

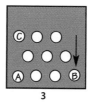

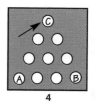

Arrow Point Trail

THE AMAZING HANDKERCHIEF

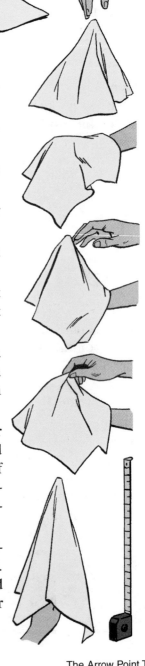

1. Spread a freshly ironed handkerchief on a table.

2. With your right hand, lift the center so that it stands by itself.

3. Lift it up to show that nothing is under it.

4. Spread the handkerchief over your left hand.

5. Lift it at the center; it stands on your hand.

6. Again, with your right hand, lift the handkerchief to show that nothing is supporting it.

7. Your left hand is concealing a mechanical tape measure, hidden by the back of your hand which is toward the audience.

8. Drape the handkerchief over your left hand. Turn your hand palm upward; grasp the end of the ruler through the handkerchief and pull out. The handkerchief will be standing in the air.

9. Push the center of the handkerchief down with the right hand. Pocket the handkerchief and metal tape measure with your left hand.

Arrow Point Trail

MAGIC DOLLAR

Say this as you fold and unfold a dollar bill: "If you had nothing to do, day in and day out, but look out of a dollar bill, you would probably think up something to do. George Washington likes to stand on his head. See?"

Hold up the bill to the audience with George Washington facing them, and follow these steps:

1. Fold the top half forward toward you (with George on the outside).

2. Fold the right half backward to the left.

3. Then fold the right half forward to the left.

4. Unfold the back half of the bill to the right.

5. Swing the front half of the bill to the left.

6. Bring the front portion of the bill upward, and old George is standing on his head.

How about that! (A new, stiff bill, or a carefully ironed old one, will make this trick easier.)

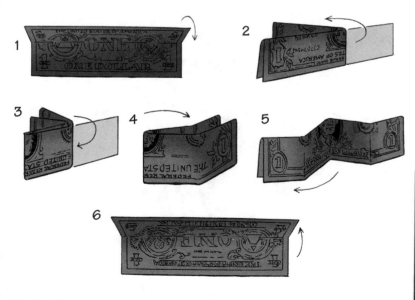

THE FLOATING BODY

Were you ever in a big crowd at a parade when you thought you saw a young boy who was taller than a grown-up? And then when you got closer you saw it was really a very small boy seated on his father's shoulders.

Well, that was an illusion. You thought you saw something strange, but it really wasn't.

Magicians use illusions all the time. One of the best is the floating body trick. With practice you can do it, too.

Here's what you need: a helper, a large bedsheet, a towel, two 3- or 4-foot-long sticks, and a pair of shoes and socks just like the helper is wearing.

Fasten the shoes and socks onto the sticks. Tie the sticks together. Roll a towel lengthwise and tie it onto the sticks to give them shape. They are supposed to be the helper's legs and should have some shape.

You will need a long, low bench that your helper can straddle. Place a cover over this so that it reaches the floor on the audience's side. The fake legs are on the floor on your side of the bench.

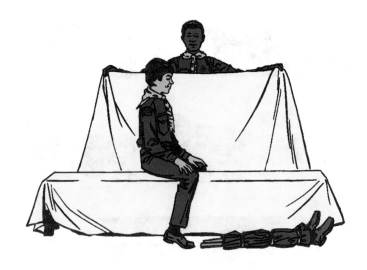

To perform the trick, follow these steps:

1. Have your helper seat himself on the bench with one leg on each side.

2. Hold the sheet to hide the bench from the audience.

3. The helper puts the false legs in place and lies backward on the bench.

4. Cover your helper with the sheet so that only his head and the fake feet stick out.

5. The helper places one hand on the bench and slowly stands up, holding his head far back, as if he were still lying down. He holds the sticks level with his other hand and raises them as he stands. This is startling if done slowly. It looks as if he is floating in air.

The trick looks hard, but with practice, the helper will be able to rise easily.

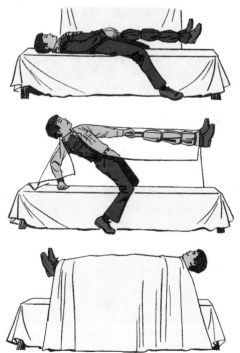

Landscaping

Some of our most useful plants are food plants. Other plants are grown for their beauty. Deciding which plants to use and how to arrange them is called *landscaping*.

Careful use of flowers, bushes, and trees can make our homes, neighborhoods, and parks nicer places to live and visit.

REQUIREMENTS

___a. With an adult, help take care of your lawn or help take care of the lawn of a public building, school, or church. Seed bare spots. Get rid of weeds. Pick up litter. Agree ahead of time on what you will do.

___b. Make a sketch of a landscape plan for the area right around your home. Talk it over with a parent or den leader. Show which trees, shrubs, and flowers you could plant to make the area look better.

___c. Take part in a project with your family, den, or pack to make your neighborhood or community more beautiful. These might be having a cleanup party, painting, cleaning and painting trash barrels, and removing ragweed. (Each time you do this differently, it counts as a completed project.)

___d. Build a greenhouse and grow twenty plants from seed. You can use a package of garden seeds or use beans, pumpkin seeds, or watermelon seeds.

NO.	DATE	ADULT SIGNATURE	✓ DEN CHART
14.			
14.			
14.			
14.			

YOUR FLOWER GARDEN

Make your flower bed interesting. Don't plant in rows but in groups as in this picture. Don't put all flowers of one kind or color in one spot. Putting light flowers in front of dark ones is the most pleasing. Plant small flowers like violets and pansies in front of taller ones like snapdragons and chrysanthemums.

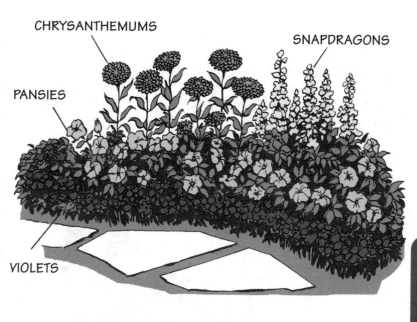

CHRYSANTHEMUMS

SNAPDRAGONS

PANSIES

VIOLETS

Plant your garden rows running as nearly north and south as possible so the plants can get lots of sun. If the ground is sloping, the rows should run crosswise, as shown. This is called *contour planting*. If the rows run uphill and downhill, rain will wash away the soil. That is called *erosion.*

SOUTH

NORTH

BEAUTIFY YOUR NEIGHBORHOOD

Help plan for a small arrangement of bushes, shrubs, or flowers around the flagpole in your schoolyard.

Maybe planting a few shrubs along the block would help make the street where you live a more pleasant place.

Why not plant the kinds of things that attract birds? Here are a few:

Bushes—Barberry, bayberry, high-bush blueberry, elderberry, mulberry, common privet, staghorn sumac, viburnum, black haw, and yew

Trees—Box elder, birch, red cedar, flowering crab, dogwood, fir, hemlock, white pine, maple, mountain ash, wild cherry, and spruce

The Arrow Point Trail

Arrow Point Trail

PLANTING SEEDS

Plant seeds in dirt. Add about 1 cup of water. Tie up and leave in a sunny spot until the seeds sprout.

Start seeds in an egg carton. Put it in a miniature greenhouse.

CLEAR
PLASTIC
BAG

SIMPLE
GREENHOUSE

POTTING SOIL
OR RICH DIRT

POTTING SOIL
OR RICH DIRT

MINIATURE GREENHOUSE

Make a greenhouse from ¾-inch wood strips. Use white glue and small box nails. Cover with heavy, clear plastic, using tacks or staples. This greenhouse fits over a cookie sheet.

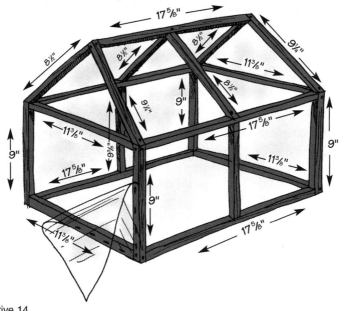

Water and Soil Conservation

Every living thing depends on clean water and rich earth. It is important that we learn as soon as we can how to care for our water and soil.

REQUIREMENTS

___a. Dig a hole or find an excavation project and describe the different layers of soil you see and feel. (Do not enter an excavation area alone or without permission.)

___b. Explore three different kinds of earth by conducting a soil experiment.

___c. Visit a burned-out forest or prairie area, or a slide area, with your den or your family. Talk to a soil and water conservation officer or forest ranger about how the area will be planted and cared for so that it will grow to be the way it was before the fire or slide.

___d. What is erosion? Find out the kinds of grasses, trees, or ground cover you should plant in your area to help limit erosion.

___e. As a den, visit a lake, stream, river, or ocean (whichever is nearest to where you live). Plan and do a den project to help clean up this important source of water. Name four kinds of water pollution.

This elective is also part of the World Conservation Award (see page 259).

NO.	DATE	ADULT SIGNATURE	✓ DEN CHART
15.			
15.			
15.			
15.			
15.			

Soil is very important to you. Almost all your food and clothing comes from plants that grow in the soil and from animals that eat those plants.

Soil covers most of the earth's land and is made up of mineral and organic particles all mixed together by wind, water, and decay.

Soils are different around the country and around the world. Soil can be different colors, depending on how much decayed organic material is part of the earth (like leaves that have fallen from trees), how damp the soil is, or which minerals are in the soil (for instance, red soil has a lot of iron oxide in it).

Soils also feel different because some are made up of larger particles than others. For instance, sandy soil is made up of bigger particles than clay. You can feel the individual pieces of sand in a sandy soil.

Layers in soil are called *soil horizons.* These horizons exist because the way the soil is formed changes throughout the soil the deeper you go. The top layers, or topsoil, is made up mostly of decaying organic matter. We grow crops in the topsoil. Below the topsoil, you may find mineral particles mixed with organic matter. The deepest layers, which are

Arrow Point Trail

not exposed to wind or much water, will be more like the original deep rocks that started the process of making soil a long time ago.

SOIL EXPERIMENT

Start with three cans the same size. Punch four holes in the bottom of each with a hammer and nail. Put clay in the first can, dirt in the second can, and sand in the third can. Fill all three cans half full. Pour a half can of water into each can, one at a time. Write down the time it takes the water to run through each kind of earth (until the dripping stops). The three kinds of earth are not good for growing things alone, but when mixed together they make very good soil.

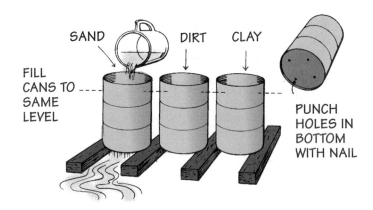

EROSION AND SOIL CONSERVATION

Soil is slowly worn away by rain, wind, and other natural forces. This is call *erosion*. But people have sometimes speeded up this natural process through activities such as building, mining, farming, and grazing.

Plants protect soil from wind and rain. Their roots hold the soil together. So clearing the land of its natural plants can be harmful to the soil and cause it to erode more quickly than new soil can be made. Sometimes, the eroded soil is deposited into lakes, streams, and rivers—polluting the water.

The Arrow Point Trail

Arrow Point Trail

Soil conservationists work with farmers and other people to make sure that soil is used wisely and too much erosion is avoided. Farmers can add organic material to the soil or plow their fields in ways that prevent erosion. Ranchers can limit the amount of time their herds graze in one area.

KEEPING WATER CLEAN

Think of all the ways you use water every day (look back at your water-usage survey from achievement 6). You will see how important water is to you, so it is also important to make sure that it is clean and safe to use.

Water can be polluted from sewage disposal, waste chemicals from industry, and runoff of soil and pesticides from farmlands. Sometimes you will hear about oil spills that pollute the ocean and also harm birds and animals. Wastewater from homes can be a major source of pollution, although communities treat their wastewater in many ways to make it cleaner.

The U.S. Environmental Protection Agency has rules about the amount and kinds of pollutants that can be dumped into lakes and streams. People are paying more and more attention to the problem of water pollution. You can do this too by trying to limit the number of detergents, chemicals, or poisons your family puts down the drain in your home.

Arrow Point Trail

Farm Animals

You can learn more about farm animals even if you don't live on a farm or a ranch. If you do, it is easier, but if not, you can find pictures of different farm animals in magazines and learn how they are used. You can read a book about farm animals. Then when you go for a ride in the country, you will know what kinds of cattle, horses, pigs, and sheep you see.

REQUIREMENTS

____a. Take care of a farm animal. Decide with your family the things you will do and how long you will do them.

____b. Name and describe six kinds of farm animals and tell their common uses.

____c. Read a book about farm animals and tell your den about it.

____d. With your family or den, visit a livestock exhibit at a county or state fair.

NO.	DATE	ADULT SIGNATURE	✓ DEN CHART
16.			
16.			
16.			
16.			

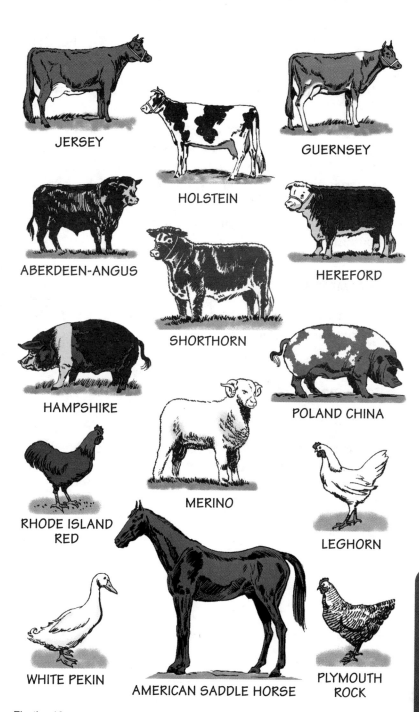

JERSEY

HOLSTEIN

GUERNSEY

ABERDEEN-ANGUS

SHORTHORN

HEREFORD

HAMPSHIRE

MERINO

POLAND CHINA

RHODE ISLAND
RED

LEGHORN

WHITE PEKIN

AMERICAN SADDLE HORSE

PLYMOUTH
ROCK

Repairs

It seems as though there is always something that needs fixing around the home. Who takes care of these repairs where you live? Maybe you have already helped with repair work. If not, ask before you try. Talk it over. Make sure you understand what to do before you start. Electrical and plumbing jobs are not games. You have to know what you're doing.

REQUIREMENTS

____a. With the help of an adult, fix an electric plug or an electrical appliance.

____b. Use glue or epoxy to repair something.

____c. Remove and clean a drain trap.

____d. Refinish or repaint something.

____e. Agree with an adult in your family on some repair job to be done and do it. (Each time you do this differently, it counts as a completed project.)

NO.	DATE	ADULT SIGNATURE	✓ DEN CHART
17.			
17.			
17.			
17.			
17.			

Arrow Point Trail

FIXING AN ELECTRIC PLUG OR APPLIANCE

With the help of an adult who is familiar with electricity, you can make repairs on light switches, sockets, and plugs. Be sure the cord is disconnected or the power is off before you start your work.

Also be sure that your hands and the floor are dry before you touch anything electrical.

PLUG

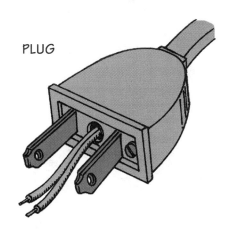

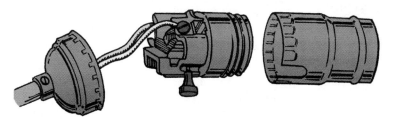

LIGHT SOCKET

HOW TO CLEAN A DRAIN TRAP

A drain trap is a J-shaped piece of pipe in a sink drain that gives a low spot to hold water. This keeps gas from the sewer from coming into the house. Sometimes it clogs up and must be taken off and cleaned out.

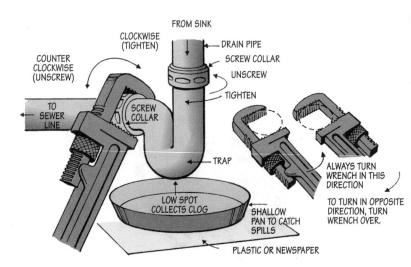

To clean a trap, first put down plastic sheeting or newspaper below the trap. The trap is full of water, so protect the area beneath the sink from spills. Use a pan to catch any drips.

Use a large pipe wrench to loosen the two screw collars that hold the trap. They have right-hand threads, which means that you turn them clockwise (the direction a clock's hands move) to tighten them. You will need to turn them the other way (counterclockwise) to unscrew them. They might be tight to start with, so you will need help from an adult with this job. After each collar has been unscrewed two or three turns with the pipe wrench, you can probably continue by hand. Be careful; the trap is full of water, soap scum, and other trapped things that you won't want to spill.

Unscrew the collars with one hand while holding the trap in the other hand so it won't fall off when the last collar lets go of it. When both collars are completely loosened, you can lift out the trap.

Carefully place the trap in the pan so it won't spill. Carry it to where you can dump it, but first remove the rubber seals. If they show signs of corrosion, you will need to replace them with new ones. The water can be poured into another drain, but the sludge and solid material should go in the trash. Flush out the trap outdoors with a hose.

Reverse the steps to replace the trap. Turn both collars at least two turns by hand to make sure the threads are matched up, and then make them as tight as you can with the pipe wrench. An adult should do the final tightening job to make the joints as leakproof as possible. Run some water in the sink to check for leaks. If you see any drips, tighten the screw collars more, or remove the trap and replace the rubber seals before putting it back.

Backyard Gym ^{ELECTIVE} 18

Have you ever visited a gym or health club? You can build your own gym in your backyard. If you don't have room, don't give up. Your den can build a gym set to use in a pack outdoor-fun day. Here are some ideas. You can find more in *Boys' Life* magazine.

REQUIREMENTS

___a. **Build and use an outdoor gym with at least three items from this list:**
   1. **Balance board**
   2. **Trapeze**
   3. **Tire walk**
   4. **Tire swing**
   5. **Tetherball**
   6. **Climbing rope**
   7. **Running long jump area**

___b. **Build three outdoor toss games.**

___c. **Plan an outdoor game or gym day with your den. (This can be a part of a pack activity.) Put your plans on paper.**

___d. **Hold an open house for your backyard gym.**

NO.	DATE	ADULT SIGNATURE	✓ DEN CHART
18.			
18.			
18.			
18.			

BANGBOARD CLOWN

On any old plank or board, paint a large clown. Cut openings for the mouth and pockets. Make them different sizes. Nail or screw a brace to the back at an angle so your clown will stand up. Toss beanbags or balls through the openings.

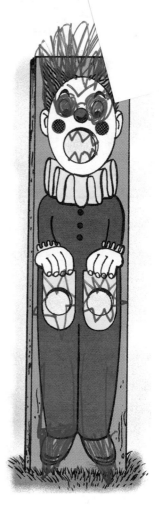

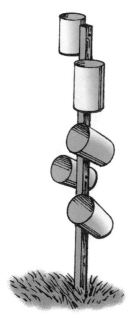

CAN CATCHER

Fasten large cans on a post. Aim some straight up and some slanting up a little. Try tossing a ball into each one. Try it from different places. This helps improve your ability to judge distance.

BOX GOLF

Set up nine cartons and number them. Throw your ball into carton 1. If you miss, throw again from where you pick up your ball. When you have gotten the ball into carton 1, throw to carton 2. Get someone to play with you.

BOX GOLF

NOTE for Akela:
Check the tires to
make sure no pieces
of wire are sticking up
through the surface.

TIRE WALK

TETHERBALL

BURY PIPE IN
GROUND TO HOLD
TETHERBALL POLE.

BACKYARD GYM

Swimming

Swimming is a lot of fun!

When you learn to swim, you have a skill you can enjoy all your life. Whether you swim for fun or for sport, you can enjoy it winter or summer and share the fun with your friends. (Remember, **never swim alone!**)

REQUIREMENTS

_____a. Jump feetfirst into water over your head, swim 25 feet on the surface, stop, turn sharply, and swim back.

_____b. Swim on your back, using the elementary backstroke, for 30 feet.

_____c. Rest by floating on your back, using as little motion as possible, for at least 1 minute.

_____d. Tell what is meant by the buddy system. Know the basic rules of safe swimming.

_____e. Do a racing dive from the edge of a pool and swim 60 feet, using a racing stroke. (You might need to make a turn.)

There is something about this elective that is different from any other. That is this rule: Whenever you are working on the Swimming elective, you must have an adult with you who can swim.

Arrow Point Trail

NO.	DATE	ADULT SIGNATURE	✓ DEN CHART
19.			
19.			
19.			
19.			
19.			

NOTE for Akela: Also see the pages on swimming in the *Cub Scout Academics and Sports Program Guide.*

FLOATING

Hold your breath. Bend down in the water and clasp your hands around your legs below the knees. Presto! You float like a cork! Stretch out your arms and legs and you will still float.

BACK FLOAT

Stretch your arms to the side and lie back in the water, letting your feet float. Hold a deep breath. The water will just cover your ears. Relax and breathe normally. This is a good way to rest in the water.

Arrow Point Trail

Basic Rules of Safe Swimming

1. Be physically fit.

2. Have a qualified adult present whenever you swim.

3. Swim in areas that have already been checked and have no deep holes, stumps, rocks, cans, or glass.

4. If you can't swim, don't go in water more than 3 ½ feet deep. If you can swim 50 feet, it's safe to go in water up to the top of your head. Go in deep water only if you are a good swimmer.

5. Swim with a buddy—someone to help you if you get into trouble, someone you can help if he needs it.

6. Obey the rules. Have a good time in the water and learn to swim a little better each time you go in.

BUDDY SYSTEM

The buddy system makes swimming safer. Every swimmer is paired with a buddy who can swim about as well as he can. Buddies stay within 10 feet of each other during the swim and check in and out of the swimming area together.

All swimmers are checked in the water about every 10 minutes. The adult in charge signals for a buddy check with a single blast of a whistle or the ring of a bell, calls "Buddies!," and counts slowly to ten while the buddies join

Arrow Point Trail

and raise hands and then remain still and silent. Guards check all areas, count the pairs, and compare the total with the number known to be in the water. Two blasts or bells is the signal to resume swimming.

At the end of the swim, a final buddy check is made and every swimmer is accounted for. Three blasts or bells is the signal for immediate checkout.

SIDESTROKE

This is a good stroke for swimming a long way because it is not very tiring.

Lie on your side in the water. Either side is okay. Your legs do what is called the scissors kick. Part them in the water as far as you can, and then bring them together as hard as you can.

At the same time, reach forward with your arm that is lowest in the water, and then pull it hard through the water back toward your body. Make a shorter stroke with your top arm as you are pulling the bottom arm back.

JUMP ENTRY

Jumping into the water feetfirst with your legs and arms spread out and forward is a safe way to enter strange waters. Don't dive if you don't know what the bottom is like. You could hurt your head or neck if the water is shallow or if there is a big rock near the surface.

Arrow Point Trail

If you are jumping from higher than 4 feet above the water, keep your feet together and your legs straight. Hold your nose with one hand as you jump.

RACING DIVE

In swimming races, you want to start fast and land in the water in a racing position. Stand with your feet slightly apart with the toes gripping the edge of the pool or dock. Crouch slightly with your arms back and your palms up.

On the signal, leap and swing your arms forward. You'll land in a swimming position.

RACING STROKE

This stroke is called the crawl. It is used for fast swims, but it can be tiring over long distances.

Arrow Point Trail

Start by floating facedown with your arms and legs extended. Begin to kick fast and evenly. Try to keep your legs straight.

As you kick, reach one arm forward as far as it will go. Then pull it back hard through the water. When it gets about halfway back, reach forward with the other arm and stroke.

To take a breath, turn your head to one side out of the water as you start to stroke with the arm on the opposite side.

ELEMENTARY BACKSTROKE

Begin by floating on your back, arms down at your sides. Bring your hands up over your chest to your shoulders. Reach straight outward and a little beyond your head. Then pull your arms back hard to your sides. At the same time you are beginning the arm movement, draw your knees out like a frog, keeping your feet together. Then spread your legs wide to the sides—just as you begin pulling your arm—and snap them together to the starting position. Breathe in through your mouth just before each stroke.

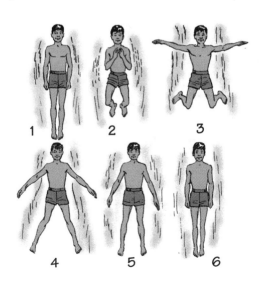

Sports

If you like sports, you aren't alone! Here are some more fun electives that will help you earn Arrow Points while you learn new sports skills. BB gun and air gun shooting is a Cub Scout activity for day camp, resident camp, and/or family camp only.

REQUIREMENTS

___a. In archery, know the safety rules and how to shoot correctly. Put six arrows into a 4-foot target from a distance of 15 feet. Make an arrow holder. (This can be done only at district/council day or resident or family camp.)

___b. In skiing, know the Skier's Safety and Courtesy Code. Demonstrate walking and kick turn, climbing with a side step or herringbone, a snowplow stop, a stem turn, four linked snowplow or stem turns, straight running in a downhill position or cross-country position, and how to recover from a fall.

___c. In ice skating, know the safety rules. From a standing start, skate forward 150 feet and come to a complete stop within 20 feet. Skate around a corner clockwise and counterclockwise without coasting. Show a turn from forward to backward. Skate backward 50 feet.

___d. In track, show how to make a sprint start. Run the 50-yard dash in 10 seconds or less. Show how to do the standing long jump, the running long jump, or the high jump. (Be sure to have a soft landing area.)

___e. In roller skating (with conventional or in-line skates), know the safety rules. From a standing start, skate forward 150 feet and come to a complete stop within 20 feet. Skate around a corner clockwise and counterclockwise without coasting and show a turn from forward to backward. Skate backward 50 feet. Wear the proper protective clothing.

NO.	DATE	ADULT SIGNATURE	✓ DEN CHART
20.			
20.			
20.			
20.			
20.			

HOW TO SHOOT WITH A BOW AND ARROW

Hold the bow level and lay an arrow across it, touching your forefinger. Nock the arrow with the cock feather turned up. Face the target sideways. As you raise the bow to a straight-up shooting position, take aim and pull the drawstring back until your hand touches your chin. Keep your left arm stiff. Release the arrow smoothly by opening your string fingers quickly.

Archery Safety Rules

• Shoot only when a grown-up is with you.
• Never nock an arrow until you're ready to shoot.
• Never aim an arrow toward anyone; point arrows only downrange, toward the target.
• When not shooting, always point the arrow downward.
• Shoot only where you have a clear view all around.

The Skier's Safety and Courtesy Code

- Ski only when properly equipped and clothed.
- Never ski alone.
- Ski under control, which means being able to turn and stop when you want.
- Ski only on slopes suited to your ability.
- Try to check the trail before skiing down it.
- Respect the rights of other skiers.
- Keep yourself physically fit.

SIDE STEP

HERRINGBONE

NOTE for Akela: Also see the pages on skiing in the *Cub Scout Academics and Sports Program Guide.*

Ice Skating Safety Rules
- Always use sharp skates.
- Skate only on approved ice surfaces in places where skating is supervised.
- Never skate alone.
- Never skate or walk on thin ice.
- Watch where you are skating at all times.
- Never throw anything onto the ice.
- Never shove or grab another skater.

Four inches of new ice is a safe thickness for a crowd. Stay ashore until the ice is tested and approved for skating. Ice is unsafe after midwinter and spring thaws.

Springs bubbling up from lake or river bottoms will prevent water from freezing. Such openings in an ice field are known as "air holes." Streams, windswept lakes, tidal rivers, and salt water are slow to freeze and dangerous except after very cold weather.

Bushes, small trees, or danger signs should be used to mark unsafe spots in daytime. Flares or lights should be used to mark them at night.

RIME AND REASON

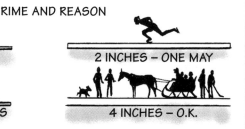

1 INCH – KEEP OFF!

2 INCHES – ONE MAY

3 INCHES – SMALL GROUPS

4 INCHES – O.K.

Roller Skating Rules for Outdoor Skating (conventional and in-line skates)

- Give pedestrians the right-of-way.
- Obey all laws about skating on the sidewalks or in the street.
- Don't race out of alleys and driveways.
- Avoid skating on chipped, broken, or rough surfaces. Watch out for rocks, branches, and trees.
- Don't skate on other people's property without their permission.
- Come to a complete stop and look in all directions for traffic before crossing streets.
- Obey traffic laws, signs, and signals.
- Don't skate in the street in traffic.
- Avoid uncontrolled coasting and skating down inclines.
- Don't hitch onto bicycles, cars, or trucks.
- Don't skate outdoors at night.
- Check your equipment before skating. Be sure all fittings are tight.
- Wear the proper protective clothing (wrist guards, helmet, knee and elbow pads).

NOTE for Akela: Also see the pages on skating in the *Cub Scout Academics and Sports Program Guide.*

SPRINT START

Because sprints are short races, a sprinter must get a fast start and run at full speed all the way.

To make a fast start, a sprinter crouches low and leans forward, with all fingers of both hands touching the ground at the starting line. One foot is far behind the other, with the heels off the ground. At the signal, the sprinter shoves off hard with the rear foot and is at full stride right away.

LONG JUMP

In the standing long jump, the jumper leaps as far as he can from the starting line into a sandpit. In the running long jump, the jumper is allowed to run up to the line before leaping.

Both standing and running long jumpers try to fall forward rather than backward when they land.

HIGH JUMP

There are two styles of high jumping. In one, the jumper approaches the bar from the side, swings the leg nearest the bar up and over, and follows with the other leg in a scissors kick.

In the other style, the jumper rolls over the bar by leaping and turning the whole body toward the bar. While going over, the jumper is looking down at the bar.

Sales

The idea of selling something goes back a long way. People were trading things even before money was invented. When people traded, they would give something for something else they wanted more. In a sale, both parties should feel that they're better off than they were before the sale. Money is an easier way of keeping track of how much things are worth.

REQUIREMENTS

____a. Take part in a council- or pack-sponsored money-earning sales program. Keep track of the sales you make yourself. When the program is over, add up the sales that you have made.

____b. Help with a garage sale or rummage sale. This can be with your family or a neighbor, or it can be a church, school, or pack event.

NO.	DATE	ADULT SIGNATURE	✓ DEN CHART
21.			
21.			

Before you sell something, check with your local council to get permission to wear your Cub Scout uniform. People should buy your product because they want it, not because you are a Cub Scout. Take pride in your appearance; remember, you are representing the entire Scouting organization.

Arrow Point Trail

Collecting Things

Many people like to collect things as a hobby. Some things that are collected are stamps, coins, and emblems. Collections are just for fun, but you can't help but learn something about other places when you find a stamp, coin, or emblem from somewhere a long way from where you live.

REQUIREMENTS

____a. **Start a stamp collection. You can get information about stamp collecting at any U.S. post office.**

____b. **Mount and display a collection of emblems, coins, or other items to show at a pack meeting. This can be any kind of collection. Every time you show a different kind of collection, it counts as one requirement.**

____c. **Start your own library. Keep your own books and pamphlets in order by subject. List the title, author, and subject of each on an index card and keep the cards in a file box, or use a computer program to store the information.**

NO.	DATE	ADULT SIGNATURE	✓ DEN CHART
22.			
22.			
22.			
22.			

Arrow Point Trail

STAMP COLLECTIONS

Boys' Life magazine has many ads for stamps and other things that can be collected. If an ad says that stamps will be sent "on approval," it means that you will have to pay for the stamps sent to you or mail them back. Some companies will give free stamps if you agree to let them send you others "on approval." You should not order these stamps unless you have enough money to buy them or pay for the postage to mail them back.

DISPLAYING A COLLECTION

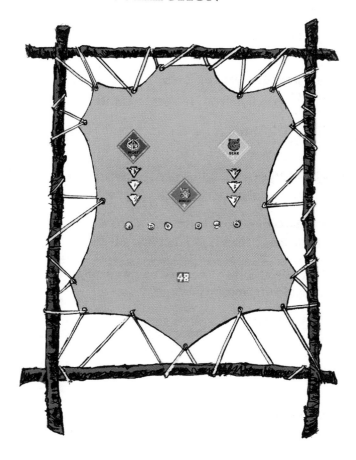

Maps

When explorers scout a new land, they make maps to show others what they find. Maps mean adventure, excitement, and imaginary trips. They are also useful for exploring your town and state.

REQUIREMENTS

___a. Look up your state on a U.S. map. What other states touch its borders?

___b. Find your city or town on a map of your state. How far do you live from the state capital?

___c. In which time zone do you live? How many time zones are there in the United States?

___d. Make a map showing the route from your home to your school or den meeting place.

___e. Mark a map showing the way to a place you would like to visit that is at least 50 miles from your home.

NOTE for Akela: Also see the pages on geography in the *Cub Scout Academics and Sports Program Guide.*

NO.	DATE	ADULT SIGNATURE	✓ DEN CHART
23.			
23.			
23.			
23.			
23.			

STATES
ALABAMA
ALASKA
ARIZONA
ARKANSAS
CALIFORNIA
COLORADO
CONNECTICUT
DELAWARE
FLORIDA
GEORGIA
HAWAII
IDAHO
ILLINOIS
INDIANA
IOWA
KANSAS
KENTUCKY
LOUISIANA
MAINE
MARYLAND
MASSACHUSETTS
MICHIGAN
MINNESOTA
MISSISSIPPI
MISSOURI
MONTANA
NEBRASKA
NEVADA
NEW HAMPSHIRE
NEW JERSEY
NEW MEXICO
NEW YORK
NORTH CAROLINA
NORTH DAKOTA
OHIO
OKLAHOMA
OREGON
PENNSYLVANIA
RHODE ISLAND
SOUTH CAROLINA
SOUTH DAKOTA
TENNESSEE
TEXAS
UTAH
VERMONT
VIRGINIA
WASHINGTON
WEST VIRGINIA
WISCONSIN
WYOMING

CAPITALS
MONTGOMERY
JUNEAU
PHOENIX
LITTLE ROCK
SACRAMENTO
DENVER
HARTFORD
DOVER
TALLAHASSEE
ATLANTA
HONOLULU
BOISE
SPRINGFIELD
INDIANAPOLIS
DES MOINES
TOPEKA
FRANKFORT
BATON ROUGE
AUGUSTA
ANNAPOLIS
BOSTON
LANSING
ST. PAUL
JACKSON
JEFFERSON CITY
HELENA
LINCOLN
CARSON CITY
CONCORD
TRENTON
SANTE FE
ALBANY
RALEIGH
BISMARCK
COLUMBUS
OKLAHOMA CITY
SALEM
HARRISBURG
PROVIDENCE
COLUMBIA
PIERRE
NASHVILLE
AUSTIN
SALT LAKE CITY
MONTPELIER
RICHMOND
OLYMPIA
CHARLESTON
MADISON
CHEYENNE

Arrow Point Trail

Native American Life

People already lived in America when Columbus got here. They were called Indians because Columbus thought he was near India. They tell many stories about where they came from, but nobody knows for sure. They hunted for their food and also grew plants that people in the rest of the world did not have. They gave us corn, squash, and pumpkins. They lived close to nature. Many tribes still have their own laws and religions.

REQUIREMENTS

____a. American Indians once lived all over what is now the United States. Find the name of the tribe that lived nearest where you live. What was this tribe best known for?

____b. Learn, make equipment for, and play two Native American games with members of your den. Be able to tell the rules, who won, and what the score was.

____c. Make a model of an early Native American house.

NO.	DATE	ADULT SIGNATURE	✓ DEN CHART
24.			
24.			
24.			

NATIVE AMERICAN GAMES

Games helped make future hunters quick of hand and sharp of eye. Try your hand at these.

MOTOWU. This is a game played by the Hopi Indians in Arizona. It's played with feathered darts made from corncobs. When you have corn on the cob, save the cobs and dry them. Cut them all to the same length, about 3½ to 4 inches, and smooth them with a piece of coarse sandpaper glued to a wood block. Make holes at both ends. Using white glue, glue a 2½-inch stick or dowel in the smaller end and two turkey feathers in the big end. You will need at least four darts.

MOTOWU

Play this game as you do horseshoes. Place two flower pots or baskets about 10 inches in diameter 12 to 15 feet apart. In turn, each player throws two darts at the same time. The darts are held in one hand with the index finger between them. You can throw directly at the basket or toss them up in the air, which makes them spin. Both darts must go into the basket; the first player to get two darts in at the same time wins the game.

POKEAN. Residents of Zuni Pueblo in New Mexico play this game. They make a kind of shuttlecock from corn husks and feathers. Save the husks from corn and dry them, but don't let them get so dry that they are brittle. Make your pokean while the husks are still soft enough to bend. You will need three corn husks 1½ inches wide and 6 or 7 inches long, and a fourth husk about ¾ inch wide and 5 inches long. Take one of the three large husks and fold it in thirds to make a pad. Lay the other two big husks on a flat surface to form a cross. Put the pad in the center of the cross. Fold the bottom husk over the top husk and the pad. Fold the top husk up and bring the ends together at the top over the center. Don't twist. Wrap the ends with the small husk. Wrap a string snugly two or three times around the ends and tie. Glue three feathers into the top with white glue. They will make the pokean twirl in the air.

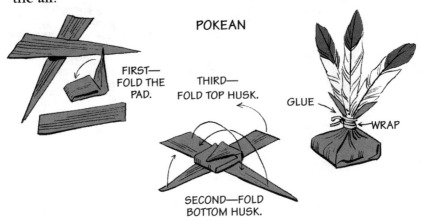

POKEAN

FIRST—
FOLD THE
PAD.

THIRD—
FOLD TOP HUSK.

GLUE

WRAP

SECOND—FOLD
BOTTOM HUSK.

Each player tries to keep his pokean in the air by hitting it with his hand. The object of the game is to count the number of times you can hit the pokean to keep it in the air before it falls. The player with the highest score wins the game.

NATIVE AMERICAN HOUSES. Native Americans built their homes to suit the kind of area where they lived. Tribes that lived on the plains built portable buffalo-skin tents called tepees. In the wet Northwest, they built wood houses with sloping roofs. Some in the Southwest built stone houses under overhanging cliffs. The Navajo lived where wood was scarce. They used short logs, bark, and earth to build cone-shaped houses called hogans. In the far North, Eskimos built houses out of snow blocks. Native Americans learned to live wherever they happened to be.

PUEBLO

HOGAN

SEMINOLE HOUSE

IGLOO

TEPEE

WIGWAM

LONGHOUSE

Getting set for
Webelos Scouting

When you have completed the third grade (or are 10 years old), you can join a Webelos den and wear the Webelos uniform.

You can earn twenty activity badges. Do you like science? You can earn the activity badges for Geologist, Scientist, and Naturalist.

Naturalist

Geologist

Scientist

Perhaps you like the outdoor life. Well, you'll find activity badges for Outdoorsman, Sportsman, Athlete, Forester, and Aquanaut.

Athlete

Forester

Outdoorsman

Sportsman

Aquanaut

There's much more. As a Webelos Scout, you also can earn the Craftsman, Engineer, Traveler, Citizen, Artist, Showman, Scholar, Communicator, Family Member, Fitness, Handyman, and Readyman badges.

Traveler

Engineer

Craftsman

Citizen

Communicator

Showman

Scholar

Artist

Family Member

Fitness

Handyman

Readyman

There are two reasons for all these activities. One is to offer you more fun. The other is to prepare you to be a Boy Scout. As a matter of fact, you will have the option of wearing the khaki/olive uniform when you become a Webelos Scout.

When you have completed the fifth grade or are age 11, or when you have earned the Arrow of Light Award, you can become a Boy Scout. You'll be ready to do that if you join the Webelos den and take part in the activities.

Some packs hold a special ceremony at the pack meeting to welcome new Webelos Scouts into the Webelos den.

How to Wear Cub Scout Insignia ___

DIRECTIONS FOR PLACEMENT

The diagrams on page 21 of this book will show you the shapes and locations of the insignia a Cub Scout will be eligible to wear.

SLEEVE INSIGNIA

All Cub Scouts, regardless of rank, wear the sleeve insignia indicated. Remove old insignia before attaching new. A Cub Scout wears only the appropriate insignia for the position he holds.

POCKET INSIGNIA

When a Cub Scout earns the Bear badge, he wears it centered on the left side of the left pocket. (See page 21.) When he earns a Gold Arrow Point, it goes ¾-inch below the Bear badge. Silver Arrow Points go directly below the Gold in two rows, as shown on page 21. The size of a Cub Scout's shirt pocket depends on his shirt size, but you will find that his Bobcat, Wolf, and Bear badges will fit easily on the average-size pocket. The Immediate Recognition Award is worn on the right pocket.

TO SEW

Use a fine overhand, back, blind, or buttonhole stitch to sew on the insignia. The thread should match the border of the emblem. When using a sewing machine, follow the manufacturer's instructions for stitching badges and emblems.

Boy Scouts of America
Cub Scout World Conservation Award

The World Conservation Award is an international award that Bear Cub Scouts can earn by doing the following things:

___ Complete Achievement 5.

___ Complete all Arrow Points in two of the following three electives:

    ___ 2. Weather

    ___ 12. Nature Crafts

    ___ 15. Water and Soil Conservation

___ Participate in a den or pack conservation project in addition to the above.

After you have done all of these things, ask your den leader to order your award.

Approved _____
                                    Akela

This award can be earned only once while
you are a Cub Scout.

Cub Scout Academics and Sports

You can have fun and learn new skills when you take part in the Cub Scout Academics and Sports program. Just by learning about and participating in a sport or academic subject, you can earn belt loops and pins.

Each Academics and Sports subject is included in the *Cub Scout Academics and Sports Program Guide*, which tells you what the requirements are for earning the special recognition of belt loops and pins.

You can take part in the program at home, in your den or pack, or in activities in your community. Ask your den leader to tell you more about the Cub Scout Academics and Sports program and the 31 Academics and Sports subjects that you can explore!

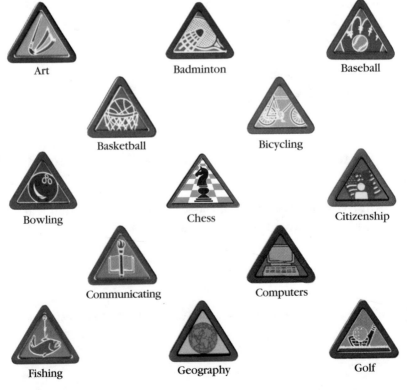

Art

Badminton

Baseball

Basketball

Bicycling

Bowling

Chess

Citizenship

Communicating

Computers

Fishing

Geography

Golf

Academics and Sports

Gymnastics

Heritages

Marbles

Mathematics

Music

Physical
Fitness

Science

Skating

Skiing

Soccer

Softball

Swimming

Table
Tennis

Tennis

Ultimate

Volleyball

Weather

Wildlife
Conservation

Bear Trail Record

To earn your Bear badge, you must complete twelve achievements. You must earn one for God (either achievement 1 or 2), three for Country (from achievements 3, 4, 5, 6, and 7), four for Family (from achievements 8, 9, 10, 11, 12, and 13), and four for Self (from achievements 14, 15, 16, 17, 18, 19, 20, 21, 22, 23, and 24).

Most achievements have several requirements. When you complete a requirement, draw a circle around the letter for that requirement on this page. When you have done enough requirements to complete the achievement, put an "X" in the box by the achievement.

If you do more requirements than you need for an achievement, you may use them for elective credit to earn Arrow Points. Mark the letter for that requirement with an "X."

On the next page, keep a list of all of your elective credits. You earn an Arrow Point for every ten elective credits you complete.

Do   **of these**

Do one for GOD

☑ 1. Ways We Worship   1   ⓐ

❑ 2. Emblems of Faith   1   ⓐ

Do three for COUNTRY

❑ 3. What Makes America Special? $a + 3$ ⓐ ⓑ ⓒ ⓓ ⓔ ⓕ ⓖ

❑ 4. Tall Tales   all 3   ⓐ ⓑ ⓒ

❑ 5. Sharing Your World with Wildlife   any 4   ⓐ ⓑ ⓒ ⓓ ⓔ

❑ 6. Take Care of Your Planet   any 3   ⓐ ⓑ ⓒ ⓓ ⓔ ⓕ

❑ 7. Law Enforcement Is a Big Job   any 4   ⓐ ⓑ ⓒ ⓓ ⓔ ⓕ ⓖ

Do four for FAMILY

☐ 8. The Past Is Exciting and Important any 3 (a) (b) (c) (d) (e) (f)

☐ 9. What's Cooking? any 4 (a) (b) (c) (d) (e) (f)

☐ 10. Family Fun both (a) (b)

☐ 11. Be Ready first 4 (a) (b) (c) (d) (e)

☐ 12. Family Outdoor Adventures any 3 (a) (b) (c) (d) (e)

☐ 13. Saving Well, Spending Well any 4 (a) (b) (c) (d) (e) (f) (g)

Do four for SELF

☑ 14. Ride Right *d* + 3 (a) (b) (c) (d) (e) (f) (g)

☐ 15. Games, Games, Games! any 2 (a) (b) (c)

☐ 16. Building Muscles all 3 (a) (b) (c)

☐ 17. Information, Please *a* + 3 (a) (b) (c) (d) (e) (f)

☐ 18. Jot It Down any 5 (a) (b) (c) (d) (e) (f) (g)

☐ 19. Shavings and Chips all 4 (a) (b) (c) (d)

☐ 20. Sawdust and Nails all 3 (a) (b) (c)

☐ 21. Build a Model any 3 (a) (b) (c) (d) (e) (f)

☐ 22. Tying It All Up any 5 (a) (b) (c) (d) (e) (f)

☐ 23. Sports, Sports, Sports! all 5 (a) (b) (c) (d) (e)

☐ 24. Be a Leader any 3 (a) (b) (c) (d) (e)

Arrow Point Trail Record

Achievement Number and Letter	Elective Number and Letter	Elective Number and Letter